100 INTERESTING FACTS ABOUT THE TITANIC

DeepCurio

Copyright © 2025 by DeepCurio

All rights reserved.

No part of this book may be reproduced in any form without the written permission of the publisher or the author except as permitted under applicable copyright laws.

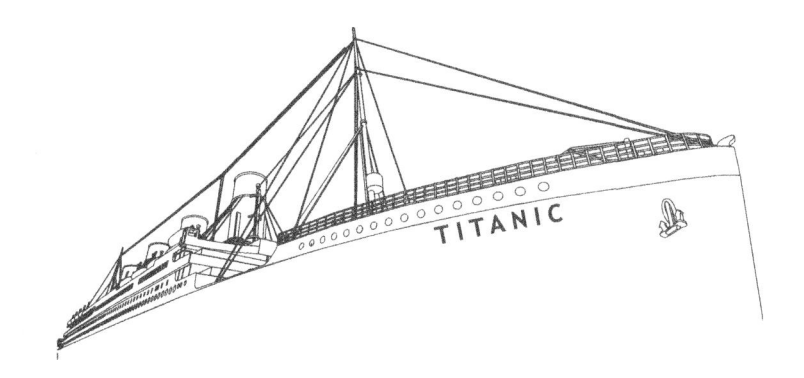

Even after more than a hundred years, there is a story that continues to resonate in the hearts and minds of those who hear it: the tale of the Titanic. It is not just the account of a journey ending in tragedy but an epic narrative filled with dreams, courage, ambition, and, ultimately, an unforgettable descent into the abyss. This book will guide you through the 100 most incredible and surprising facts about that event, revealing little-known details, hidden stories, and curiosities that may elude even the most devoted enthusiasts of this history.

From the beginning, you will step into the shipyard, where the most famous ship in the world comes to life. The construction of the Titanic was not just an unprecedented engineering feat but also a symbol of modernity, humanity's defiance of nature's forces, and progress. In these pages, you will uncover the secrets behind its steel walls, the men who built it, and the decisions that, perhaps, could have changed the ship's fate.

But the Titanic wasn't just a marvel of engineering; it was a floating city, a luxurious home for the world's wealthiest, and a beacon of hope for thousands of emigrants seeking a new life. You will immerse yourself in life onboard, exploring the opulence of first class, the vibrancy of third class, and the dedication of the crew. What was it like to live on that legendary ship? How did the passengers spend their days, unaware of the tragic fate that awaited them?

The pages of this book are filled with extraordinary characters, heroic figures, and stories of sacrifice. From Captain Edward Smith, who stayed at his post until the very end, to the unsung heroes who gave everything to save others, each story is an essential piece of this voyage. You'll also discover lesser-known individuals who, while not as famous, played an important role in shaping the Titanic's legend.

Then, inevitably, you'll arrive at that fateful night. The tragedy that turned a ship into a myth. You'll read accounts of the moment the Titanic struck the iceberg, the panic that spread as water began to flood its lavish halls, and the stories of those who survived and those who did not return. Through these accurate and incredible facts, you'll feel like you're there, among the cold Atlantic waves, experiencing every moment with emotion.

The journey doesn't end there. After the sinking, the Titanic remained shrouded in mystery, hidden in the depths of the ocean for decades. In this book, you'll trace the most fascinating discoveries made by researchers and explorers who illuminated what the sea had kept hidden for so long. You'll uncover surprising finds, artifacts that tell the stories of those onboard, and theories that still surround this legend today.

And finally, like every great story, the Titanic's tale is wrapped in intrigue and mystery. Conspiracy theories, strange coincidences, and unusual facts are ready to keep you hooked until the last page. There is always something new to learn about the Titanic, and this book will take you to the heart of these mysteries.

But there's more. This book isn't just a collection of facts; it's an immersive experience. After discovering the 100 incredible facts, you'll have the chance to test your knowledge and observational skills with an exclusive bonus section specially designed to make your journey into the world of the Titanic even more exciting and engaging. You'll challenge yourself, uncover new details, and gain access to extra content that will surprise you even further. But I won't reveal everything now; the best awaits you within these pages.

100 Interesting Facts About the Titanic is not just a book. It's your opportunity to relive one of the most fascinating and tragic stories in human history. Prepare to set sail with me aboard a ship that, despite everything, has never stopped navigating our hearts.

FORGING THE LEGEND

Luxury and Legend: The Birth of the Titanic

At the beginning of the 1900s, the ship was the only way to cross the ocean. Two British companies, Cunard and White Star Line, competed for passengers. In 1907, Cunard completed the Lusitania and the Mauretania, fast ships that crossed the Atlantic in just five days. White Star Line's response? Build three ships, not the fastest, but the largest and most luxurious in the world: the Olympic class ships.

The idea was born in London during a dinner in 1907 at the home of Lord Pirrie, chairman of the Harland & Wolff shipyard, with J. Bruce Ismay, director of the White Star Line. They decided to build the Olympic, the Titanic, and the Gigantic (later renamed Britannic).

Although British, the Titanic was financed by J.P. Morgan, the powerful American banker and founder of General Electric. Thanks to Morgan's funds, the dream of building the most luxurious ships in the world became a reality.

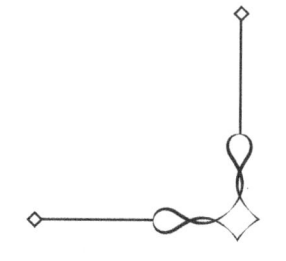

A Giant of the Seas: The Titanic's Extraordinary Dimensions

Have you ever tried to imagine just how enormous the Titanic was? Get ready to be amazed. The Titanic was 882 feet long, practically the length of two football fields placed end to end. Its width measured 92 feet, wider than three buses lined up side by side.

From the keel to the top of the funnel, the height reached 174 feet, almost as tall as a 15-story building. But that is not all. It weighed around 51.000 long tons, combining the weight of over 5,000 elephants.

It was the largest ship of its time. Think about that the next time you see an elephant at the zoo. The Titanic could virtually carry thousands of them. No wonder it remains one of the most famous and fascinating ships in history to this day.

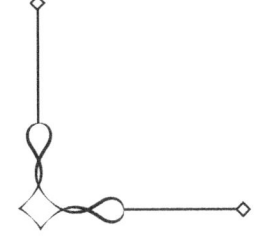

The Naming Choice: Mythology and Majesty

Did you know that the name "Titanic" was chosen to evoke the image of the Titans, legendary giants from Greek mythology? It was meant to symbolize something immense. Additionally, all ships of the White Star Line, a company renowned for luxury and innovation, had names ending in "-ic" (like Baltic and Oceanic), while those of their rival, Cunard Line, known for speed, ended in "-ia" (like Mauretania and Lusitania). The Titanic was no exception.

But there's more: the prefix "RMS" stood for "Royal Mail Ship," signifying that the Titanic carried royal mail between the United Kingdom and the United States. This meant the Titanic wasn't just a passenger vessel. It also transported critical correspondence and high-value telegrams. The ship even had a dedicated section for sorting and processing mail, making it prestigious for its luxury and vital role in essential services.

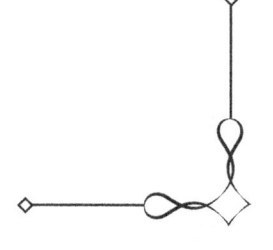

The Titanic's Five Flags: Symbols of Luxury and Fate

During its famous maiden voyage, the Titanic flew five flags, each carrying a special meaning. On April 11, 1912, after departing from Ireland, the Titanic raised the American flag on the foremast, signaling its final destination was the United States. With 46 stars, it represented the states at the time.

On the main mast, the flag of the White Star Line, the Titanic's owner, waved proudly, while at the stern, a flag from the British Admiralty displayed the ship's British connection, along with the captain and crew.

The Royal Mail flag also granted the Titanic its status as a Royal Mail Ship, giving it privileges in ports. Finally, the Blue Peter flag marked "All aboard!" as the Titanic set sail from Queenstown.

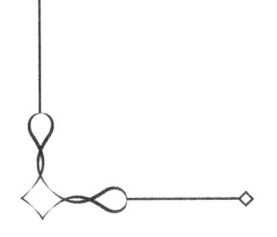

The Birth of a Giant: Two Years of Challenges and Tragedies

In the 1910s, building a ship like the Titanic was difficult and dangerous. In just two years, 15,000 men worked at the Harland & Wolff shipyards, facing harsh conditions without modern safety measures such as helmets or gloves.

This led to significant risks, with 246 recorded injuries, 28 of which were serious, including amputated arms and crushed legs. Tragically, six workers died directly on the ship, while two others lost their lives in the shipyard workshops.

The workers endured shifts from 7:50 AM to 5:30 PM, five days a week, earning around ten dollars per week, roughly equivalent to 230 dollars today. The construction of the Titanic not only created legends but also required immense sacrifice.

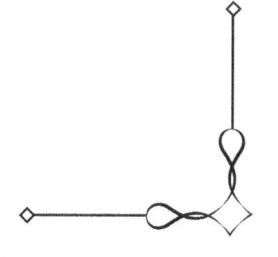

When the Cold Revealed the Limits: The Hidden Weakness of Iron Rivets

The shipyard used approximately three million rivets to assemble the Titanic, many of which were made of iron rather than steel, a choice that proved problematic. Some of these rivets contained high concentrations of slag, an impurity that made them particularly fragile. Compared to steel rivets, iron ones were less durable and especially vulnerable to the low temperatures of the Atlantic Ocean.

The ship's about 1-inch thick steel plates were designed to provide solid protection. However, the weakness of the iron rivets, worsened by the extreme cold of the Atlantic Ocean, compromised the overall integrity of the structure.

This structural issue would have significant effects under extreme stress, contributing to the ship's reduced robustness.

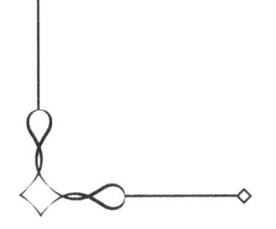

Designing the Impossible: The Ship That Was Meant to Be Unsinkable

Imagine building a ship that everyone believes to be invincible. This is exactly what happened with the design of the Olympic-class ships. With a cost of approximately 7.5 million dollars at the time, equivalent to around 180 million dollars today, the ship was a masterpiece of engineering.

One of its most innovative features was the double-bottom hull, designed to provide extra safety. The ship was divided into 16 watertight compartments, creating a kind of protective barrier.

This design allowed the ship to stay afloat even if up to four compartments were flooded, contributing to its reputation as "unsinkable." With this system, the idea was that even in the event of serious emergencies, the ship could continue to sail.

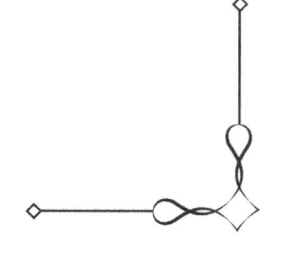

The Beginning of a Legend: The Titanic's Launch

The launch is the moment when a ship is put into the water for the first time. The Titanic was launched on May 31, 1911, as an enormous empty shell with incomplete interior details. More than 100,000 people gathered at the Harland & Wolff shipyards and along the River Lagan to witness this spectacular event.

At the time of its launch, the ship weighed 25,000 long tons. The 738-foot wooden platform on which it was built was greased with 20 long tons of animal fat, soap, and train oil to make it slippery.

The Titanic slid into the water in 62 seconds, slowed by heavy chains and mooring cables. Unfortunately, worker James Dobbin lost his life during the launch, crushed by a wooden beam that had been holding the ship in place.

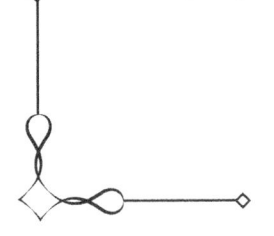

Giants of Steel: The Titanic's Anchors and Propellers

The Titanic had three massive anchors: two side anchors, each weighing 23 feet, and a central anchor that, at 46 feet, was the largest ever built at the time. No fewer than 20 horses were needed to transport this enormous central anchor.

The ship was also equipped with three powerful propellers. The two side propellers, each with three blades, had a diameter of 23 feet and weighed 34 tons. The central propeller, with four blades, measured 16 feet in diameter and weighed 20 tons.

These propellers worked together to propel the Titanic to a cruising speed of 22 knots. These figures not only highlight the ship's grandeur but also reflect the technological innovation of the time. For instance, lifting and positioning these anchors and propellers required advanced equipment and techniques for that era.

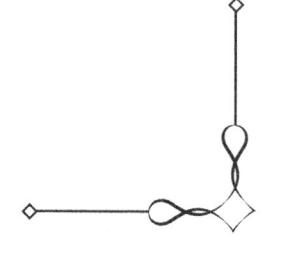

The Engine: A Miracle of Engineering

The Titanic was a marvel of engineering, with engines that weighed nearly 427 tons and generated 16,000 horsepower. The crankshaft alone weighed 130 tons, measured 12 feet in diameter, and 13.7 feet in length.

Coal fueled 29 boilers to generate steam, which powered the triple-expansion engines connected to the two side propellers, enabling them to complete up to 75 revolutions per minute. The residual steam then powered a turbine that spun the central propeller at 165 revolutions per minute. Afterward, the steam passed into a condenser, which converted it back into water to be redirected into the boilers.

With a coal capacity of 6,600 tons, the Titanic consumed approximately 640 to 850 tons per day to maintain a speed of 22 knots, making each voyage an extraordinary feat of energy and logistics.

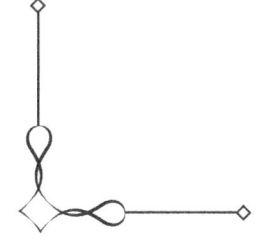

Technology and Luxury: How Electricity Worked Onboard

The Titanic featured an advanced electrical system for its time. Four main generators, connected to the Parsons turbine, produced 400 kilowatts each, generating a direct current of 16,000 amps at 100 volts. Altogether, the ship's power station generated approximately 2,300 horsepower, supplying a network of electrical cables 200 miles long and powering around 10,000 light bulbs.

To ensure safety in case of an emergency, two auxiliary generators of 30 kilowatts each were also located on Deck D.

Thanks to this system, the Titanic glowed with electric light and had enough power to operate all its vital systems, from lights to kitchens, making the journey a luxurious and comfortable experience for all passengers.

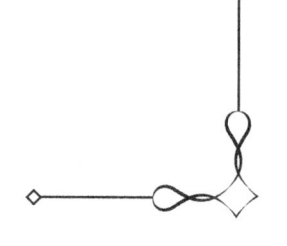

The Secret of the Titanic's Imposing Funnels

The Titanic's funnels were truly impressive. Each funnel measured 62 feet in height, 22 feet in width, and 23 feet in length.

Although only three funnels were necessary for properly operating the ship's boilers, a fourth was added to make the vessel appear even more majestic. This additional funnel was not connected to the boilers but served to ventilate the ship's interior and expel fumes from the kitchens and the first-class smoking room chimney.

Thanks to this fourth funnel, many ventilation shafts could be removed from the decks, making the ocean liner's design even more elegant and streamlined. The funnels, therefore, enhanced the ship's functionality and added to its grandeur and aesthetic appeal.

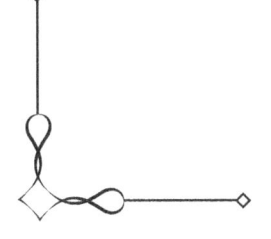

Invisible Waves: Morse Code on Board the Titanic

Did you know that the Titanic featured a revolutionary technological innovation for its time? Onboard was the Marconi wireless telegraphy system, which allowed messages to be sent via radio waves using Morse code.

This special code, composed of dots and dashes representing letters and numbers, was used for communication between ships. The Titanic's Marconi room, located just behind the bridge, was the hub for these transmissions.

Passengers could even send personal messages, though it wasn't cheap: three dollars for the first ten words and thirty-five cents for each additional word! This system helped maintain communication between ships and played a crucial role during the emergency on the night of the sinking.

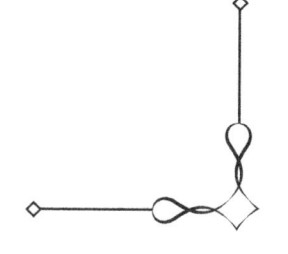

Fatal Elegance: The Mystery of the Titanic's Lifeboats

Did you know the Titanic had only 20 lifeboats, enough for 1,178 people? Although the ship could carry over 3,500 passengers and crew, lifeboats were reduced for aesthetic and deck space reasons.

The architects wanted to preserve the ship's elegant appearance and provide more room for strolling, so they chose not to add additional lifeboats.

It was also believed that the Titanic, considered "unsinkable," would sink slowly in an emergency, allowing enough time for everyone to be rescued by other ships. While there were enough life jackets, many lifeboats were launched half-empty. This miscalculation contributed to the tragic loss of numerous lives that night.

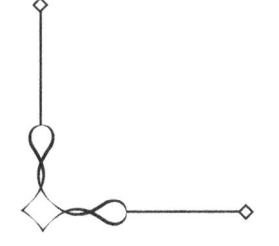

Sailing Between Confidence and Haste: Shortened Sea Trials

Like cars, ships must be tested before carrying passengers, and the Titanic was no exception. On April 2, 1912, tugboats guided it to sea for a series of essential trials: turning to the right (starboard) and left (port), sudden stops, and speed tests at various levels. These trials were initially planned to last several days, but they were completed in less than 24 hours due to bad weather and strong winds.

The builders were confident: the Titanic's sister ship, the Olympic, had passed all its tests without issue, so it was assumed the Titanic would be equally ready to sail. Despite the shortened trials, they were deemed sufficient to ensure the ship's safety, and nothing was expected to delay its official departure scheduled for April 10, 1912.

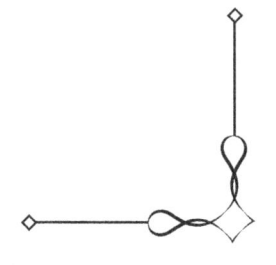

LUXURY ON THE OCEAN

From Extreme Luxury to Survival: The Price of Dreams Aboard

On the Titanic, ticket prices varied significantly depending on social class. A standard first-class ticket cost $146 at the time, which translates to approximately $5,000 today. For those seeking the ultimate luxury, a first-class suite was priced at $4,200, equivalent to an astonishing $145,000 today.

Second-class passengers could enjoy a comfortable journey for $63, around $2,000 today. Meanwhile, a third-class ticket cost $34, roughly $1,200 today, representing hope and sacrifice for a brighter future.

These prices highlighted the stark social divisions of the era, with wealthy passengers indulging in unimaginable luxury while third-class travelers embarked on their voyage with optimism and resilience.

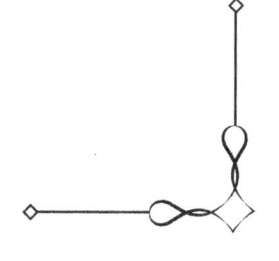

Faithful to the End: A Love for Animals on the Titanic

Owning a dog aboard the Titanic was a privilege reserved exclusively for first-class passengers. According to a 2012 exhibit at Widener University, 12 dogs were officially registered on the ship, though it is believed that some passengers may have brought animals secretly, without documentation.

Tragically, only three of these dogs survived the disaster: two Pomeranians and a Pekingese, who were rescued along with their owners on lifeboats.

One of the most touching stories of animals on the Titanic involves Ann Elizabeth Isham. According to legend, she refused to abandon her beloved dog. She chose to stay with him until the end, turning this account into a poignant symbol of loyalty and love for animals.

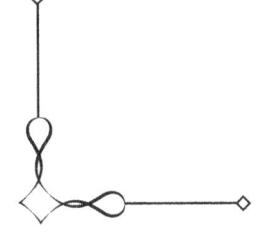

The Hierarchy of Luxury: Life and Divisions Aboard the Titanic

In 1912, the Titanic epitomized the strict social and gender divisions of the era. The first-class smoking room was an exclusive space reserved for men, as public smoking by women was deemed inappropriate. Women, instead, enjoyed the privacy of a writing room designed specifically for them, featuring white paneled walls and elegant furnishings. Though technically open to everyone, it was rare for men to venture into this refined space.

These distinctions extended beyond gender to social class. Second-class passengers were allowed to explore first-class areas only before the ship departed; afterward, they were confined to their designated sections. For third-class passengers, the experience was even more segregated. They were housed in modest accommodations located at the ship's stern, entirely separate from the higher classes, which was a stark reflection of the rigid social hierarchy of the time.

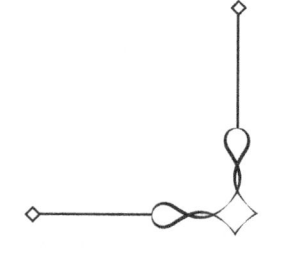

Entertainment at Sea: Luxury and Leisure Aboard a Giant

Onboard the Titanic, entertainment was remarkably diverse and innovative for its time, offering activities tailored to all social classes. First-class passengers could enjoy a swimming pool located on Deck F, one of the earliest pools ever installed on a ship. Access cost 25 cents, with men scheduled to swim in the morning and women in the afternoon. On Deck G, a squash court was available for 50 cents, along with a gymnasium on the boat deck for those interested in physical fitness. Social pastimes included card games, chess, checkers, or simply relaxing on deck chairs along the promenades.

Second-class passengers experienced a warm, communal atmosphere. They could play cards, dominoes, or chess in smoking rooms or libraries and take advantage of dedicated outdoor spaces for relaxation and conversation. For third-class passengers, evenings were often filled with music and dancing in the common rooms. They also enjoyed card games or spent time socializing on benches at the ship's stern. The Titanic aimed to provide entertainment and recreation for all passengers, reflecting its ambition to be a luxurious floating city that catered to a wide array of needs and tastes.

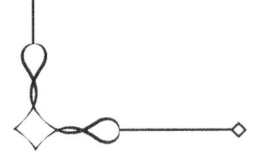

The Staircase of Luxury: The Majestic Heart of a Maritime Icon

Standing 60 feet tall, the famous Grand Staircase was the true centerpiece of Titanic's first class. It was a masterpiece of elegance. Positioned between the first and second funnels, it stretched from the boat deck down to E deck. Natural light streamed through a grand glass and wrought iron dome, illuminating hand-carved oak paneling.

At the center of the first landing, a carved clock featured the design of "Honor and Glory Crowning Time." Inspired by the 17th-century English style, the staircase was adorned with floral motif railings that added to its opulence. At its base stood a statue of a cherub holding a torch, ready to greet guests grandly.

Surrounding the staircase were blue upholstered sofas and chairs that enhanced the luxurious ambiance. Behind it were three elevators, providing a convenient way for passengers to move effortlessly between decks.

This architectural marvel was not just a staircase. It symbolized the Titanic's unparalleled grandeur and attention to detail.

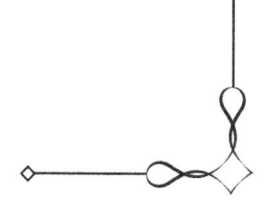

From Luxury to Tradition: The Secrets of Titanic's Kitchens

The Titanic's kitchens were a true marvel of culinary engineering, designed to cater to every class with an impressive variety of high-quality dishes. First-class passengers enjoyed exquisite meals served in luxurious French-style restaurants, prepared by an extensive team of chefs and a staff 62 dedicated solely to food preparation.

The first and second-class kitchens occupied an entire section of D Deck, spanning nearly 165 feet. They were equipped with two massive cooking ranges, nineteen ovens, and cutting-edge appliances such as rotisseries, grills, and ice-making machines, ensuring impeccable service. A dumbwaiter system connected the kitchens to refrigerated storage areas for added convenience.

Even third-class passengers experienced excellent dining services, supported by advanced kitchen equipment for the era. The onboard bakeries produced high-quality Viennese bread for all classes, ensuring a culinary experience that matched the Titanic's reputation for luxury and innovation.

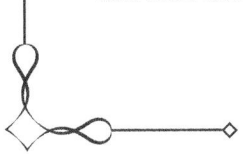

Culinary Excellence: The Lavish Feast of the Titanic's Last Supper

On the evening of April 14, 1912, what would become the final dinner aboard the Titanic took place, a luxurious event held in the Ritz restaurant, considered the most elegant dining venue on the ship. First-class passengers, unaware of the tragic fate that awaited them, delighted in an extraordinary menu. The ten courses featured refined appetizers such as oysters, consommé Olga, and barley cream, followed by sumptuous main dishes like fillet, mint-crusted lamb, and chicken lyonnaise. The dinner continued with roasted squab and foie gras, concluding with desserts like chocolate éclairs and pudding. That dinner had become legendary for its opulence and because it was the last meal served before the ship sank. The original menus were recovered from the wreck, and today, many people attempt to recreate those dishes inspired by cookbooks available on platforms like Amazon.

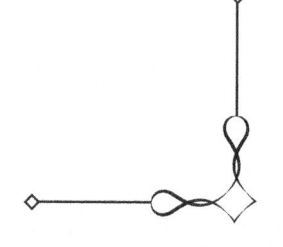

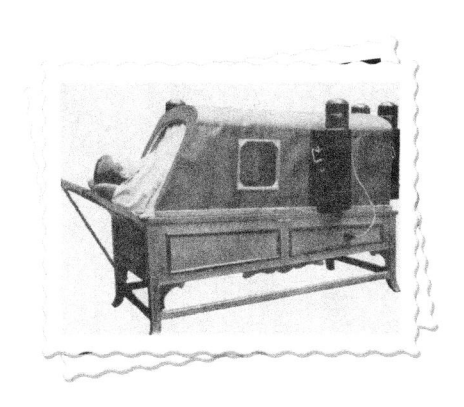

Light Therapy: A Luxury Treatment Aboard the Titanic

At the beginning of the 1900s, the idea that "light therapy" could cure numerous illnesses spread widely. It was believed that exposure to light, especially ultraviolet light, could treat conditions like scurvy, chronic gastritis, constipation, and even obesity. This therapy became so popular that special departments were created in hospitals. Electric baths were considered a true luxury, and the Titanic was equipped with one for first-class passengers. The Olympic, its sister ship, even had two. However, by the 1940s, it was discovered that ultraviolet light had no real curative effects on many illnesses. As a result, electric baths gradually disappeared, giving way to more modern and scientifically proven therapies.

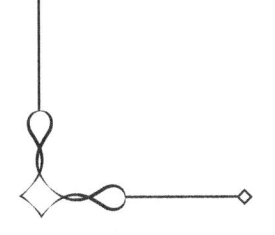

Doctors and Miracles: The Story of the Hospital at Sea

On board the Titanic, there was a surprisingly advanced hospital for the time, comparable to those found in small British or American medical centers. First-class passengers received an informational manual with details about an experienced doctor, Dr. William O'Loughlin, who was in charge of the entire medical team. Alongside Dr. John Simpson and a group of nurses, O'Loughlin inspected the crew and checked the health of third-class passengers before boarding to prevent the spread of contagious diseases. Each passenger was issued a personal medical file.

The hospital was divided into areas for first, second, and third-class passengers and the crew. Interestingly, three Syrian children were turned away for health reasons but were thus saved from the shipwreck. The hospital offered care to everyone, regardless of class.

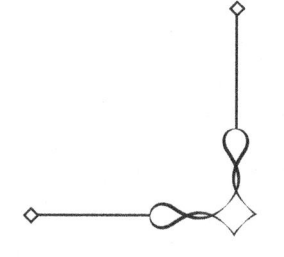

Class and Bathing: How Luxury Was Divided Among Travelers

Sanitary comforts varied greatly depending on the ticket class on the famous ocean liner. First-class passengers had access to luxurious suites with private bathrooms and porcelain bathtubs. Even Captain Smith had his own personal bathtub with both hot and cold water.

In the third class, things were far simpler: only two bathtubs, one for men and one for women served hundreds of people. Everything had to be kept clean by the stewards responsible for disinfecting the facilities.

Interestingly, third-class toilets were automatic, unlike those in first and second class, as it was believed that less affluent passengers were not accustomed to flushing toilets. Public restrooms were also available, and a special luxury soap called Vinolia was even provided in first class.

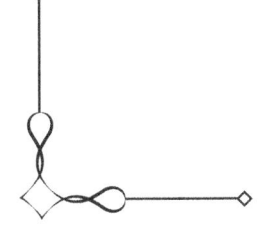

FACES OF THE LEGEND

The Invisible Heroes: The Crew Who Kept the Legend Afloat

The crew of the Titanic was an extraordinary team of 892 people who, behind the scenes, kept the most famous ship in history alive. From the 73 deck officers who ensured safe navigation to the 325 engine room workers immersed in the heat of the boilers, every role was essential. Then there were the 494 stewards, always ready to serve passengers with a smile in a world of unparalleled luxury. Salaries told different stories: a stoker earned £6 per voyage, while a waiter received only £3. Cooks earned £20, and musicians £4 for accompanying the elegant evenings. The chief engineer earned as much as £35, but Captain Smith bore the greatest responsibility with his £105 monthly salary. Among the crew were also 23 women and youths as young as 14, small heroes of the sea.

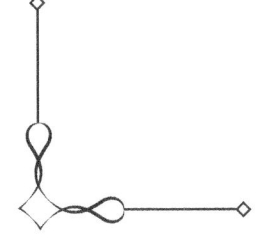

Master of the Seas: The Story of the Legendary Captain Smith

Edward J. Smith, born on January 27, 1850, in Hanley, became one of the most experienced and respected captains of his time, ultimately chosen for a legendary role: commanding the Titanic on its maiden voyage. After starting as a sailor at the age of 13, Smith joined the White Star Line in 1880, and by 1895, he had taken command of the Majestic, which he led skillfully for nine years. Considered the best captain for the world's largest and most luxurious ships, he was selected to command first the Olympic and then the Titanic, the largest ship ever built. His salary was £1,250 per year, equivalent to around $170,000 to $180,000 today, plus a £200 bonus (approximately $25,000 to $30,000) if he avoided accidents. At 62 years old, after 38 years of service, Smith was ready to retire immediately after that fateful voyage.

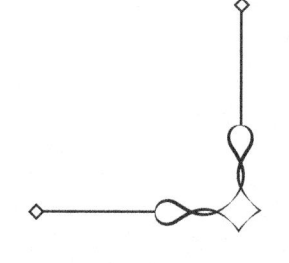

Melodies Upon the Waves: The Silent Heroes of the Shipwreck

The orchestra aboard the Titanic was comprised of eight brave musicians divided into two groups. One performed in the À la Carte restaurant, while the other, led by Wallace Hartley, played in the ship's grand salons. These musicians were talented classical music performers and adept at playing the popular ragtime rhythms of the era. In exchange for room, board, and a small wage, their task was to entertain passengers with melodies that made each evening feel special. But on the night of April 14, 1912, as chaos spread aboard, the orchestra chose to continue playing. Even after all the lifeboats had been lowered, the musicians remained at their posts, delivering a final, poignant concert until 1:40 a.m., when the Titanic was about to sink. It was an act of extraordinary courage that has forever marked history.

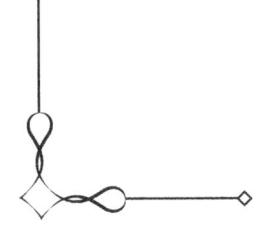

Miss Unsinkable: The Extraordinary Life of Violet Jessop

Violet Constance Jessop, born on October 2, 1887, near Buenos Aires, is a true legend of the sea. At just 21 years old, she began working as a stewardess for the White Star Line aboard the *Olympic*. But Violet was no ordinary worker: she survived all three incidents involving the famous sister ships. First, the *Olympic* in 1911, when it collided with the cruiser HMS *Hawke*. Then, the tragic sinking of the *Titanic* in 1912, and finally, the sinking of the *Britannic* in 1916, where she was serving as a nurse. Despite these harrowing experiences, she continued her maritime career for 40 years. Violet, nicknamed "Miss Unsinkable," recounted her incredible story in memoirs published in 1998. Her extraordinary ability to endure danger has immortalized her name among the legends of the sea.

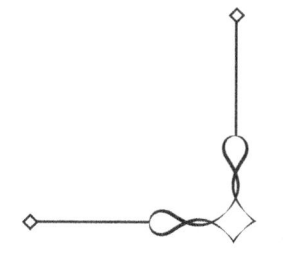

The Titanic Lookout: The Story of Frederick Fleet and the Iceberg Tragedy

Frederick Fleet, born in 1887 in England and raised at sea after becoming an orphan, served as a lookout aboard the Titanic on the night of April 14, 1912. His responsibility was to spot dangers, and when he saw the iceberg, he immediately raised the alarm. However, the ship struck the iceberg and began to sink, and despite desperate efforts, the tragedy could not be avoided. Fleet survived, but the guilt haunted him for the rest of his life. He believed a pair of binoculars might have allowed him to spot the iceberg sooner and perhaps change the ship's fate. This belief tormented him, making him a tragic figure in the Titanic's story. His name remains a symbol of human fragility and the heavy emotional toll of the disaster, a lasting reminder of the struggle against fate and guilt.

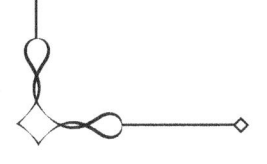

The Whiskey Captain: The Dramatic Survival of Charles Joughin

Among the Titanic survivors, Charles Joughin, the ship's chief baker, became famous for his daring escape from death. After the ship struck the iceberg, Joughin oversaw the distribution of bread and assisted with the boarding of women, refusing a spot on the lifeboats to set a good example. Later, he threw around fifty deck chairs into the sea to provide flotation support for those struggling in the water. Amidst the chaos, Joughin drank several generous sips of whiskey. When he finally plunged into the freezing waters of the Atlantic, he was nearly completely intoxicated. He swam for about two hours before finding the overcrowded Collapsible Lifeboat B. When the lifeboat was finally rescued, Joughin was still alive and later claimed he hadn't suffered much from the cold. He died in 1956 and is remembered as a symbol of resilience and courage.

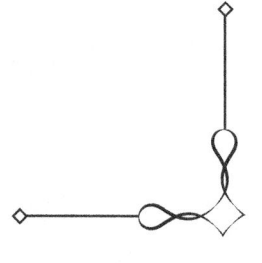

Thomas Andrews: The Man Who Stayed to Help and Accepted His Fate

Thomas Andrews, the architect of the Titanic, embodied true courage and dedication. On board to oversee the maiden voyage, Andrews stayed until the very last moment to help passengers, displaying extraordinary calm and dignity. Instead of seeking safety for himself, he devoted his time to guiding and comforting those in need, reflecting his commitment to the safety and well-being of others. As depicted in the film Titanic, Andrews helped passengers and accepted his fate with remarkable serenity. His bravery and selflessness remain a beacon of heroism, reminding us of the sacrifice and humanity of those who never abandoned their sense of duty in the face of tragedy.

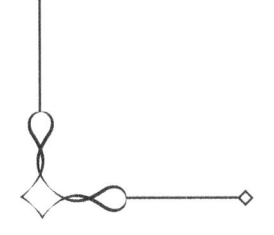

Jack Phillips: A Beacon of Hope Who Never Left the Radio Room

Jack Phillips, the Titanic's wireless operator, is remembered as a hero for his bravery and dedication on the fateful night of April 14, 1912. Alongside his colleague Harold Bride, Phillips stayed at his post in the radio room, sending desperate distress signals as the ship sank.

Even as water flooded the radio room, Phillips continued transmitting emergency messages, using every bit of power left. His tireless determination was critical in coordinating rescue efforts and saving many lives. Tragically, Phillips, only 25 years old, perished along with the Titanic, meeting his fate beneath the waves.

His sacrifice and unwavering commitment are a powerful example of heroism and dedication to the end. Today, his memory symbolizes courage and selflessness in the face of unimaginable disaster.

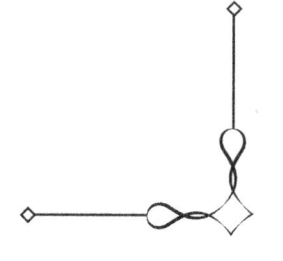

Dreams and Premonitions: When Passengers Felt Their Fate

Some passengers aboard the Titanic experienced unsettling premonitions before the tragic sinking. Officer Wilde, for instance, wrote to his sister: "I don't like this ship; I have a strange feeling about it." This dark foreboding tragically came true. Survivor Eva Hart, who was only seven years old at the time, recalled how her mother, gripped by an unexplainable fear, stayed awake every night of the voyage, convinced that something terrible was about to happen. Even far from the ocean, some families of passengers reported having distressing nightmares on the very night of the disaster, dreaming of people drowning. These premonitions, though inexplicable, add a layer of mystery and unease to the already tragic story of the Titanic, reminding us how fate sometimes seems to announce itself in subtle and mysterious ways.

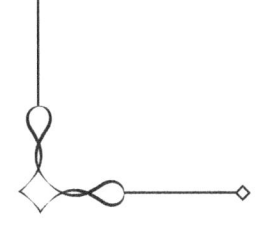

The Vast Fortunes Lost in the Icy Atlantic

Among the first-class passengers aboard the Titanic was an extraordinary concentration of immense wealth. It is estimated that their combined fortunes were valued at around 600 million dollars at the time, equivalent to approximately 9.8 billion dollars today. The first class was home to magnates, entrepreneurs, and members of the newly rich, representing the global elite of the era. Among them were figures who left their mark on history, including prominent businessmen and philanthropists. Despite their economic power, the disaster spared no one, not even the wealthiest. Only a third of the first-class passengers survived that tragic night, a sobering reminder that in the face of such tragedies, money loses all meaning. This catastrophe showed how fate made no distinction between social classes, rendering the Titanic tragedy a universal lesson for all humanity.

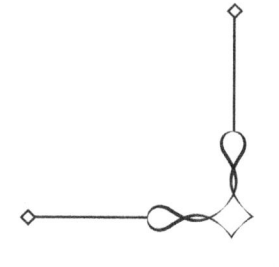

The Richest Man on the Titanic: How His Watch Still Captivates

John Jacob Astor IV, the wealthiest passenger aboard the *Titanic*, had a fortune estimated at 87 million dollars at the time, equivalent to billions today. He was renowned for constructing the iconic Waldorf Astoria Hotel in New York, which remains famous today. Astor and his pregnant wife, Madeline, boarded the *Titanic* at Cherbourg in the spring of 1912 to escape the public criticism surrounding their controversial marriage. Madeline survived, while Astor remained on the ship until the very end. His body was recovered on April 22nd, wearing a 14-carat gold pocket watch engraved with his initials, JJA. Today, this watch, still in possession of the Astor family, stands as a symbol of fine watchmaking and one of the rarest artifacts, a precious reminder of the *Titanic* and its enduring legacy.

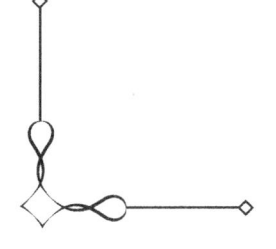

The Heartbreaking Story of Benjamin Guggenheim

Benjamin Guggenheim, born in New York on October 26, 1865, inherited a vast fortune from his father, Meyer, a mining magnate. In 1912, following a stay in Paris, he had planned to return to America aboard the *Lusitania*, but a mechanical issue forced him to change his ticket and board the *Titanic* instead. Accompanied by his valet, Victor Giglio, and his lover, Mrs. Aubart, he departed from Cherbourg.

After the collision, steward Henry Samuel Etches convinced Guggenheim to put on a life vest and head to the deck. However, Guggenheim, hesitant to face the chaos, returned to his cabin. There, he changed into his finest evening attire and declared with a statement of timeless class: *"We are dressed in our best and are prepared to go down like gentlemen."*

Guggenheim and Giglio perished in the disaster, while Mrs. Aubart survived. The image of Guggenheim and his valet, dressed as if for the *Titanic's* final ball, remains a haunting symbol of quiet dignity and composure, one last act of greatness in the ship's darkest hour.

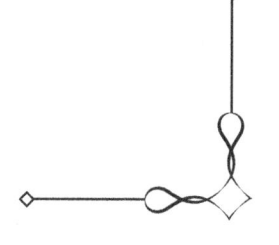

The Heartbreaking Choice of Ida Straus on the Titanic

Isidor Straus, co-owner of Macy's, and his wife Ida embody one of the most touching stories of the *Titanic*. Born to be together, they faced even their final tragedy side by side. On the fateful night of the sinking, Ida was offered a spot on a lifeboat, but upon seeing that Isidor was not allowed to board, she chose to remain with him.

Isidor, a true gentleman, refused his place, stating that he would never take the opportunity of survival from a woman or child. Despite repeated insistence, he stood firm in his decision.

Ida, filled with love and loyalty, refused to leave him alone. *"We have been together for 40 years,"* she said, *"and where you go, I go."*

Despite their courage, neither survived that tragic night. Isidor's body was later recovered, but Ida's was never found, forever cementing their legend.

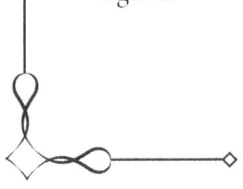

The Forgotten Story of the Countess of Rothes

Lucy Noel Martha Leslie, Countess of Rothes, was a true heroine on the tragic night of the *Titanic*. Born on December 25, 1884, she married the 19th Earl of Rothes in 1900. When she boarded the *Titanic* in Southampton, she traveled to Vancouver with her maid and cousin.

After the collision with the iceberg, the Countess found herself aboard Lifeboat No. 8 alongside other women. However, instead of remaining passive, Lucy courageously took control of the situation: she grabbed the oars and began steering the boat, calmly guiding the other survivors toward safety.

The sailor Thomas Jones, moved by her strength and leadership, removed the lifeboat's identification plaque and gave it to the Countess as a token of gratitude.

The two maintained an affectionate connection for years, exchanging letters every Christmas until the Countess passed away on September 12, 1956.

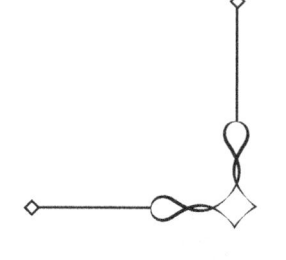

The VIPs Who Traveled in Luxury and Faced a Tragic Fate

Dorothy Gibson, a celebrated silent film actress, was aboard the *Titanic* with her mother, Pauline. Born in New Jersey in 1889, Dorothy rose to fame thanks to her talent as a model and actress, starring in over twenty silent films.

After a vacation in Europe in 1912, she boarded the *Titanic* on April 10, occupying cabin E22. When the ship struck the iceberg, she described the moment as a "sickening crunch." Dorothy and her mother managed to escape by boarding Lifeboat No. 7.

A month later, Dorothy became even more famous with the film *Saved from the Titanic*, based on her real-life experience. This cinematic success cemented her celebrity status and was also her final film.

Dorothy spent the rest of her life away from the spotlight, living in Europe until she died in 1946 in Paris.

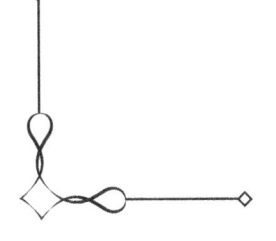

THE NIGHT OF DESTINY

Destiny at Sea: The Titanic's Endless Journey

The Titanic, the giant of the seas, set sail on April 10, 1912, from Southampton, England, embarking on an epic transatlantic voyage to New York, one of the most coveted passenger routes of the era. After brief stops in Cherbourg, France, and Queenstown (now Cobh), Ireland, the oceanic titan ventured into the vast Atlantic.

The journey spanned approximately 2,870 nautical miles (3,300 mi), and the Titanic, cruising at 21-22 knots, covered 386 nautical miles (around 444 mi) on its first day. Passengers, surrounded by an atmosphere of luxury, were filled with the excitement of the voyage.

In the following days, the ship maintained an impressive pace, with its arrival in New York scheduled for April 17. Yet, a subtle unease lingered in the air, a foreboding of the unforeseen events that would abruptly end this unparalleled adventure on the night of April 14-15.

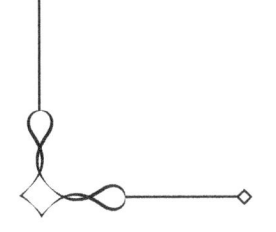

The Titanic's Iceberg: Evidence Rediscovered After 100 Years

Growlers are small ice fragments, usually less than 6 feet in height, that break off from larger icebergs. It is believed that the iceberg that struck the Titanic stood about 59 feet tall, just slightly above the height of the lifeboat deck. An extraordinary photograph resurfacing after over a century may capture this very block of ice.

Captain W. Wood of the SS Etonian took the image on April 12, 1912, just 40 hours before the Titanic met its tragic fate. The coordinates recorded by Wood match those of the disaster. He sent the photo to his great-grandfather and a letter stating, "This is the iceberg that sank the Titanic."

Although various images of icebergs have surfaced over the years, this one is considered the most credible due to its shape, which matches the descriptions provided by survivors. A piece of history frozen in time immortalized forever.

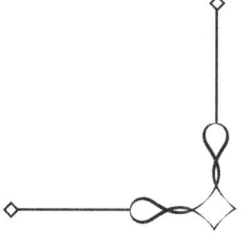

The Mysterious Scent of Ice: Warnings from the Iceberg

Imagine standing in the crow's nest of the Titanic on a calm, icy night. Fredrick Fleet, the lookout who first spotted the iceberg, didn't have binoculars, yet some sailors believed they could smell ice before seeing it. This fascinating notion comes from the words of Archie Jewell, another lookout, who claimed that one could sense an iceberg before approaching it.

Icebergs are ancient blocks of ice that sometimes contain fragments of trees, animals, and other organic materials frozen within. As they melt, they release an unpleasant odor that, carried by the wind, might be detected by sailors.

Elizabeth Shutes, a passenger, recounted that the night the Titanic struck the iceberg, the air had a peculiar scent, almost like the caves of a glacier she had visited in Switzerland. Despite this, neither Fleet nor the others could spot the danger in time.

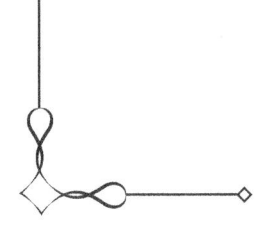

Signals from the Deep: The Morse Code the Titanic Missed

Ships like the Titanic communicated via radio waves using Morse code, a system of dots and dashes representing letters and numbers. This method was employed to transmit messages from the Marconi Room, located behind the ship's bridge.

Crucial messages requiring the captain's immediate attention had to include the prefix MSG (Master Service Gram) to ensure they were delivered directly. However, several telegrams warning of icebergs lacked this designation and, as a result, were not given the appropriate priority.

Captain Edward Smith placed his trust in the lookouts and the prevailing visibility conditions, stating that if the weather worsened, he would reduce the ship's speed. Nevertheless, he had unwavering faith that the lookouts would spot any potential dangers in time to avoid obstacles, including the icebergs that loomed as silent threats to their journey.

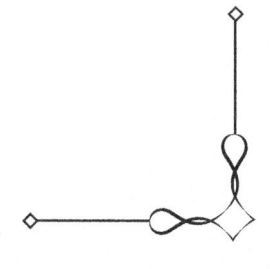

The Titanic's Final Vigil: The Iceberg Drama

Frederick Fleet rang the bell three times, signaling the presence of an iceberg straight ahead of the Titanic. "Iceberg, right ahead," he relayed to the bridge. First Officer Murdoch reacted swiftly, ordering "Full astern" and instructing helmsman Robert Hitchens to turn the wheel hard to starboard while simultaneously activating the switch to close the watertight doors.

Their hearts racing, the officers watched helplessly as the ship drew closer to the looming obstacle. Despite their efforts, it was too late; a grinding noise reverberated through the starboard side of the ship. Had the Titanic turned just a few degrees more, disaster might have been averted.

The first five compartments and part of the sixth were severely damaged. With four compartments flooded, the ship was doomed to sink. After the collision, an anxious Captain Smith asked, "What have we struck?" Murdoch replied, "An iceberg, Sir."

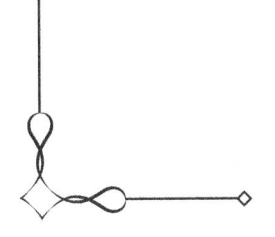

The Key to Fate: An Object, A Tragedy

The story of the British liner might have had a very different ending. A key left in the pocket of an officer who stayed ashore altered the ship's destiny. Had it been aboard, the lookouts could have unlocked the locker to retrieve the binoculars and spotted the iceberg in time.

David Blair, the second officer, left the Titanic at the last moment, unknowingly taking the key with him and failing to hand it over to his replacement. In a postcard to his sister-in-law, he expressed his disappointment at missing the maiden voyage, unaware of the tragic implications of his oversight.

One of the few survivors, Fred Fleet, believed the key could have saved many lives. Today, that simple object has become a symbol of what might have been sold at auction in 2007 for £90,000.

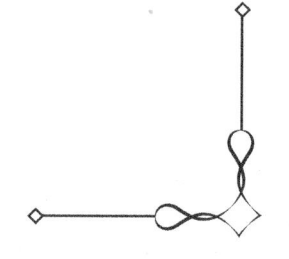

Head-On Impact: Ships and the Game of Chance

Maritime history and mythology intertwine when discussing collisions between ships and icebergs. Not all collisions are fatal: the SS Arizona, 450 feet long, struck an iceberg in 1879 and remained in service for another 50 years. Similarly, the SS Grampian suffered significant damage in 1919 but did not sink.

Had the Titanic faced the iceberg head-on, the impact might have awakened all passengers and enabled a quicker evacuation, especially given that the 20 lifeboats were insufficient for everyone on board. The theory suggests that a frontal collision would have distributed the forces more evenly, reducing the risk of multiple compartments flooding.

The Titanic's steel honeycomb structure at the stern could have absorbed the shock more effectively, increasing the ship's chances of survival.

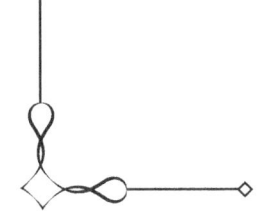

The Secret Revealed: The Iceberg's Impact on the Titanic

For years, it was believed that the iceberg caused a 295-foot gash along the Titanic's hull. However, when Robert Ballard discovered the wreck in 1985, he observed that the riveted plates were dented and scraped, not "cut." The rivets had popped, allowing water to flood the ship. When the director of the White Star Line heard the sound of the iceberg scraping along the hull, he assumed it was a propeller blade breaking.

He rushed to the bridge to ask Captain Smith if there was serious damage. The reply was ominous: "I'm afraid so." The engineers frantically worked to pump out the water, but the flooding was too severe. Thomas Andrews declared that the ship would sink within an hour and a half.

At 12:10 a.m., wireless operator Jack Phillips sent the first SOS message in history as the Carpathia raced to their aid 57 miles away.

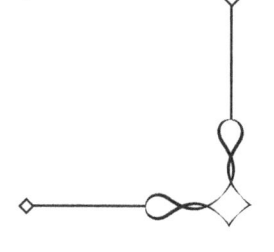

The Tragic Misstep: Errors and Fate at Sea

The Titanic did not sink solely due to the iceberg's impact but also because of a tragic steering error. Helmsman Robert Hitchens misunderstood the order to turn right and, following old sailing techniques steered the ship in the wrong direction.

This "secret" was revealed by Louise Patten, granddaughter of Second Officer Charles Herbert Lightoller, who kept silent to protect the careers of his colleagues. Unfortunately, the chain of errors did not end there: after the collision, Captain Smith, under pressure from Joseph Bruce Ismay, decided not to stop the ship, which led to even more water flooding in.

Had the Titanic remained stationary, the water would have been more contained, allowing the ship's watertight compartments to slow the flooding and increase the chances of rescue. Many more lives could have been saved before the ship sank.

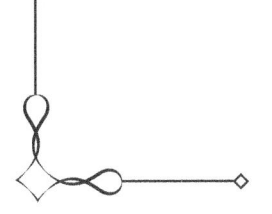

Salvation Denied: The Lifeboats That Weren't Enough

The stewards calmly notified first-class passengers, advising them to wear warm clothing and life vests and proceed to the lifeboat deck, carefully avoiding panic. In third class, many passengers, like Carl Jonsson and Daniele Buckley, did not need any warnings their cabins were already flooded.

The Titanic was equipped with 14 main lifeboats, each with a capacity of 65 people, 2 emergency lifeboats for 40 people, and 4 collapsible wooden and canvas boats for 47 people each, providing a total capacity of 1,178 seats.

However, approximately 1,029 people were left without any chance of survival that night. Despite technological advancements and the increasing size of ships, the outdated 1894 regulations required only 16 lifeboats for vessels over 10,000 tons. Initially, many passengers refused to believe the Titanic could sink and hesitated to board the lifeboats, making the evacuation even more challenging.

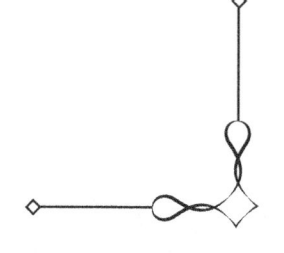

Signals of Hope: The Truth About the Titanic's Flares

In the chaos of the night when the Titanic sank, every flare shot into the sky symbolized a desperate call for help. The signal flares, fired to draw the attention of nearby ships, became a beacon of hope for passengers and crew. However, confusion about their colors sparked debates for decades.

The first flare was fired at 12:55 AM, followed by eight more at regular intervals. For years, there was uncertainty about whether they were all white or of different colors. Conflicting eyewitness accounts added to the mystery until a 2012 expedition unearthed a box containing the original flares.

It was revealed that these flares had brass tips with colored buttons, confirming that flares of various colors, including blue, red, and green, were used, as they were standard for signaling maritime emergencies.

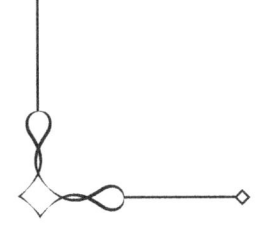

Lifeboats and Gunshots: The Struggle for Survival

With the Titanic doomed, by around 1:15 AM, the water had reached the ship's name engraved on the bow. The lifeboat boarding process grew increasingly frantic as the deck began to tilt more steeply. By 1:30 AM, the first signs of panic emerged among the passengers.

While lowering lifeboat no. 14, which carried 60 people, including Fifth Officer Lowe, some men tried to leap from the deck into the boat. To maintain order, Lowe fired three warning shots into the air. By then, over 1,500 people were still aboard, desperate, as the Titanic's propellers began rising out of the water.

The tragedy had become inevitable, marking the end of an era of blind faith in technology and safety.

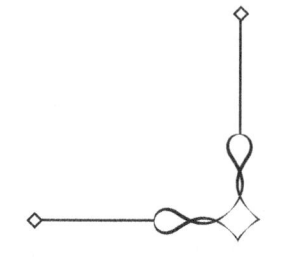

The Final Concert: Music That Defied Death

As the Titanic sank into the Atlantic, panic spread rapidly among the passengers, with desperate screams blending with the sound of the sea. Amid this chaos, the ship's orchestra stood out for its extraordinary bravery, playing until just minutes before the ship went under, around 2:00 a.m.

Despite the increasingly steep incline of the deck, the musicians continued to perform to maintain calm among the passengers, offering them one final fragment of serenity.

Some survivors recalled hearing "Nearer, My God, to Thee," while wireless operator Harold Bride mentioned "Autumn," a popular waltz of the time.

In that dreadful atmosphere, filled with music and despair, the heroic gesture of the musicians remained etched in the memories of those who managed to survive the tragedy.

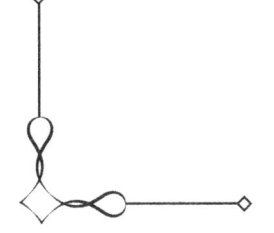

The Broken Giant: The Tragic End of an Era

Until the wreck was discovered in 1985, it was believed the Titanic had sunk in one piece. However, many survivors, including Jack Thayer, claimed that the colossal ship had broken in half. The structural stress on the hull was unbearable, especially in the rear section where the heavy engines and turbine were located. The break occurred just ahead of the third funnel at a ventilation shaft that weakened the structure.

Estimates suggest that the ship descended at a speed of approximately 31-37 phm as it sank. At that velocity, it reached the seabed in about four minutes. The stern, after tilting backward, rose vertically before completely detaching. This dramatic moment occurred at 2:20 a.m. on April 15, 1912.

What transpired during those 160 minutes continues to captivate the world's imagination.

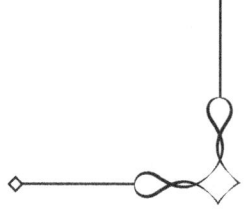

Faith in the Darkness: The Priest of the Titanic

Father Thomas Roussel Davids Byles, an English Catholic priest, boarded the Titanic with a second-class ticket, bound for New York to officiate his cousin's wedding. On the morning of April 14, 1912, during a Mass held for second and third-class passengers, he could not have foreseen the tragedy that lay ahead. When the sinking began, Father Byles displayed remarkable courage: he helped countless passengers board lifeboats, twice refusing a spot for himself.

In the end, he gathered a group of passengers at the stern of the ship, reciting the rosary, hearing confessions, and offering absolution in a moment of despair. That was the last time he was seen. His body was never identified, but his act of faith and bravery remains etched in collective memory.

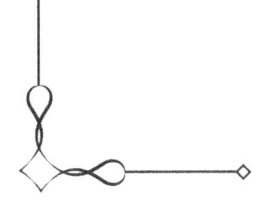

The Leap of Desperation: Lives Shattered in the Ocean

During the sinking, the survival instinct drove many passengers to leap into the sea from staggering heights, some as high as 131 feet, in a desperate bid to save themselves. Faced with the rapid submersion of the ship, escaping became the only thought, even though the height made such jumps incredibly dangerous.

The impact of the water from such altitudes was devastating, often causing severe injuries. In some cases, the force was so violent that passengers fractured their necks or sustained other fatal injuries. Additionally, the life vests, filled with cork, often exacerbated the situation upon hitting the water.

The sudden buoyant force could jolt their bodies upward, snapping their necks and killing them instantly. Although instinct compelled them to jump in an attempt to escape the sinking ship, the dangers posed by the height and inadequate equipment proved fatal for many.

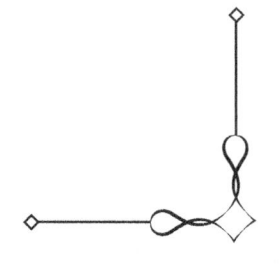

20 Minutes Between Life and Oblivion: The Grip of Hypothermia

On that fateful night, the waters of the North Atlantic were around 28°F, a lethal temperature for anyone who fell in. Despite the extreme cold, the water had not frozen due to its salinity, which lowered the freezing point.

In such conditions, the human body initially begins to shiver in an attempt to generate heat, but as the core temperature continues to drop, the shivering ceases. The heart rate slows, breathing becomes shallow, and profound fatigue sets in. The mind grows confused, leading to unconsciousness and, ultimately, death by hypothermia.

At these temperatures, a person can survive for an average of only 15-20 minutes before their body succumbs. Survivors in the lifeboats recalled hearing the desperate cries gradually fade until there was nothing but silence. By 3 a.m., the sea was enveloped in an eerie and haunting stillness.

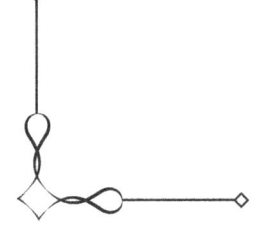

The Woman Who Defied the Ocean: The Incredible Molly Brown

Molly Brown was in Lifeboat No. 6, under the command of Quartermaster Hitchens, who refused to turn back to rescue those struggling in the water. Agitated, he berated the passengers, especially Molly, and insulted the men at the oars for their rowing technique.

But Molly Brown, determined and fearless, refused to be intimidated. She shouted at Hitchens to leave the helm to a woman and join the men at the oars. When he refused, she grabbed an oar herself, encouraging the other women to do the same.

When the Carpathia appeared on the horizon, Hitchens insisted the ship wasn't coming to save them, further terrifying the passengers. Frustrated and exasperated, Molly threatened to throw him overboard. Her heroic actions earned her the nickname "The Unsinkable Molly Brown," celebrated in books and films as a symbol of resilience and strength.

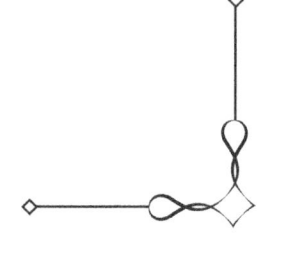

The Ship That Defied the Ice: The Rescue That Saved 705 Lives

On the night the Titanic sank, the Carpathia, a Cunard Line vessel, was carrying only 743 passengers despite having a capacity of 2,550. Having departed from New York on April 11, 1912, it was bound for the Mediterranean.

When Captain Rostron received the distress signal from the Titanic, aware of the presence of icebergs, he ordered the lookouts doubled and machinery and heating systems turned off to gain speed, pushing the ship from 14 to nearly 18 knots.

To rescue the survivors, men were hoisted aboard using rope ladders, women with hammock-like chairs, and children in netted sacks. The rescue operations lasted more than five hours, saving 705 people. The Carpathia took three and a half days to reach New York, docking on April 18, 1912, marking the conclusion of one of the greatest maritime rescue missions in history.

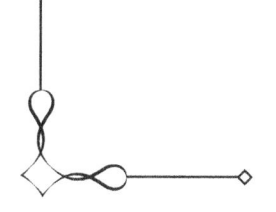

Flares in the Darkness: The Mystery of the Ignored Ship

One of the most enigmatic elements of the Titanic tragedy was the ship Californian. According to some survivors, as the Titanic sank, they saw flashes of a ship on the horizon, seemingly stationary. The Californian warned the Titanic of ice hours earlier, but the liner ignored its message. The Californian's radio operator switched off the equipment at 10:40 PM to go to bed, leaving the Titanic's subsequent distress signals unanswered.

Shortly after midnight, an officer aboard the Californian, while on deck, noticed several white flares and mistook them for shooting stars. He reported them to the captain, who attempted unsuccessfully to establish visual contact. For years, Captain Stanley Lord was accused of failing to provide assistance.

However, later studies suggested that there might have been a third, mysterious ship between the Californian and the Titanic, which ignored all emergency signals.

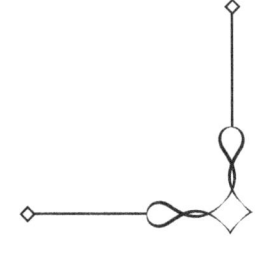

THE SECRET OF THE DEPTHS

Remembering Those Who Never Returned

The White Star Line dispatched the steamship Mackay-Bennett from Halifax on April 17 to search for those who had not survived the disaster. Over nine days of searching, the crew found many people still wearing life jackets, describing them as peacefully asleep.

Identifying the victims proved difficult in some cases, so ceremonies were held at sea, marked by prayers and solemn respect. Others were identified through personal effects such as documents, wallets, or items bearing their initials. Altogether, 328 individuals were recovered, and 59 were returned to their families.

The rest were laid to rest in three cemeteries in Halifax: Baron de Hirsch, Fairview, and Mount Olivet, where they remain to this day. The mission of the Mackay-Bennett stands as a poignant testament to the respect and remembrance of those who never made it home.

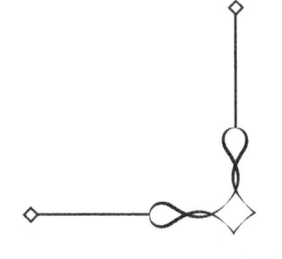

Lives Lost and Hopes Shattered: The Fate of Passengers and Crew

In the tragic sinking, survival rates varied dramatically by class. Of the 329 first class passengers, 199 managed to survive. Only 119 out of 285 passengers were saved in the second class, while in the third class, a mere 174 out of 710 people survived. The toll on the crew was devastating: out of 899 members, 685 perished.

Being classified as "deaths on duty," the crew's families received no compensation. However, charitable organizations such as the Titanic British Relief Fund managed to raise £450,000 to support those most affected, while $261,000 was collected in the United States.

Although claims for damages totaled $17 million, the final settlement amounted to just $663,000. This tragic outcome not only marked the loss of human lives but also ignited a prolonged struggle for aid and support for the devastated families.

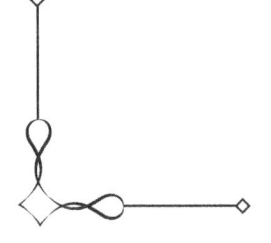

Beyond the Sea: The Untold Stories of the Survivors

No remaining survivors of the Titanic disaster exist today, but their stories endure. Millvina Dean, the youngest passenger at just two months old, passed away in 2009. Charles Lightoller, the ship's Second Officer, became a hero in the British Navy during World War I. Harold Lowe, the Fifth Officer, continued his naval career until 1944. Frederick Fleet, the lookout who first spotted the iceberg, led a troubled life and passed away in 1965.

Harold Bride, the ship's radio operator, went on to work in communications during World War I. Arthur Rostron, captain of the rescue ship *Carpathia*, was celebrated and honored for his bravery. Stanley Lord, captain of the *Californian*, was accused of failing to provide timely aid, though many defended him, believing he had been made a scapegoat.

The lives of these individuals, ranging from heroes to figures of controversy, left an indelible mark on history and remain an integral part of the story of one of the sea's greatest tragedies.

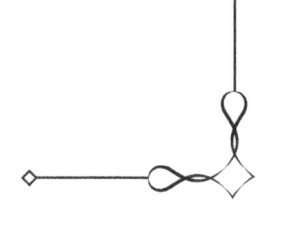

The Bulwark of the Seas: The Astonishing Story of the Olympic

The *Olympic*, the twin ship of the renowned *Titanic*, had a successful history before the tragic event that overshadowed its fame. However, after the disaster, safety became a top priority. On April 24, 1912, the *Olympic*'s stokers went on strike, refusing to depart without a sufficient number of lifeboats.

Ticket sales plummeted, and the White Star Line temporarily withdrew the ship from service for extensive modifications. The hull was reinforced, and 48 additional lifeboats were added, bringing the total to 68. During World War I, the *Olympic* was converted into a troop transport ship, ferrying 119,000 soldiers across the ocean.

It survived four attacks by German submarines and sank a U-boat, earning the nickname "Old Reliable" for its dependability and resilience during the conflict. A truly legendary ship in every sense.

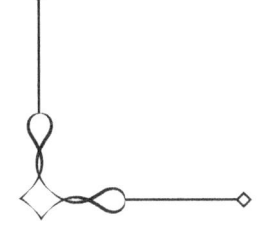

Between Innovation and Tragedy: The Voyage of the Britannic

The Britannic, the "third sister" of the famous White Star Line ocean liners, represents a captivating blend of luxury and innovation, tragically marked by an unexpected fate during World War I.

Following the sinking of the Titanic, the White Star Line decided to change the name of its sister ship from Gigantic to Britannic. Launched on February 26, 1914, the Britannic promised even more luxurious interiors, featuring elaborate decorations and a grand staircase equipped with a pipe organ. Designed with advanced safety features, such as a double-hulled structure and taller watertight bulkheads, the Britannic never had the chance to serve as a passenger ship.

In 1914, it was requisitioned and converted into a hospital ship. Tragically, on November 21, 1916, while sailing near the island of Kea, a violent explosion struck its bow, causing the ship to sink in just 55 minutes. Fortunately, only 30 of the 1,100 people onboard lost their lives. The wreck was later discovered by Jacques Cousteau in 1976.

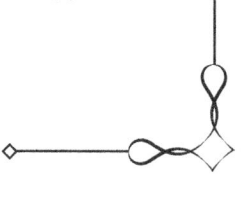

The Titanic Rediscovered: Ballard's Journey to Uncover a Lost Giant

Robert Ballard, a renowned explorer and marine geologist, is celebrated for his extraordinary discoveries in the depths of the ocean. Even before finding the *Titanic* in 1985, Ballard had distinguished himself through explorations of hydrothermal vents on the Pacific seabed and his role in locating historic military wrecks. His work has opened new frontiers in oceanographic research, employing advanced technologies such as robotic submarines.

On September 1, 1985, Ballard located the *Titanic* at a depth of 12.500 feet in the Atlantic. His discovery, long sought after and attempted by many, was a moment of immense elation, quickly followed by the sobering realization, in his own words, of standing before a massive graveyard.

Ballard and his team were the first to closely examine the wreck of the great liner, a feat achieved in just 12 days. This accomplishment cemented his reputation as one of the greatest explorers of our time.

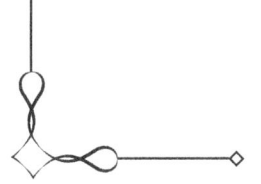

Beyond the Wreck: How Robert Ballard Conquered the Challenge

In 1982, Robert Ballard sought funding from the U.S. Navy to develop robotic submarines, which were essential for his quest to locate the *Titanic*. The Navy agreed but on one condition: Ballard first had to locate two American submarines lost during the Cold War, the *Scorpion* and the *Thresher*. Successfully completing the mission, he was left with just 12 days to search for the *Titanic*.

Ballard employed a groundbreaking strategy, focusing on the debris trail left by the wreck rather than the ship itself. On the night of September 1, 1985, his underwater cameras captured an image of one of the *Titanic*'s boilers. After months of relentless effort, the discovery had finally arrived.

The following year, Ballard explored the wreck using the *Alvin* submersible, uncovering that the *Titanic* had broken in two. His achievement was not just a technological triumph but also a heartfelt tribute to the victims of the tragedy.

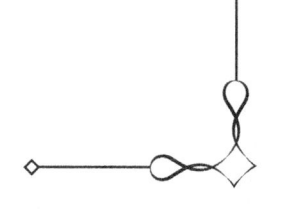

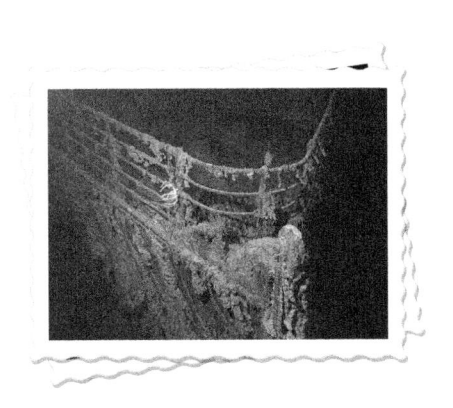

Shadows of Iron and Crystal: Exploring the Titanic

While exploring the *Titanic*, Robert Ballard described the wreck as "an endless wall of black iron rising from the seabed." The ship, covered in reddish, stalactite-like formations, was more than just rust: these were "rusticles," colonies of anaerobic bacteria feeding on the iron's minerals.

Using a robot named Jason Junior, Ballard ventured inside the ship, discovering that the crystal chandeliers were still hanging while mollusks had devoured the wood. The ship is split into two sections; its stern and bow are 2000 feet apart. The stern, partially imploded during its descent to the seabed, still displays its massive engines and some of its propellers.

Ballard unveiled a submerged world of mystery and decay, where the *Titanic* rests ruined but not forgotten. His exploration brought to light a wreck that continues to tell its tragic story.

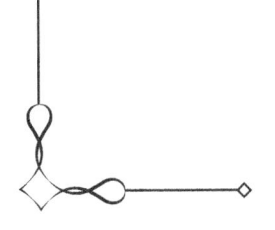

From the Depths: The Secrets of a Wreck Unveiled

No human remains have ever been found on the wreck. Over time, the passengers' bodies completely decomposed in the calcium carbonate-deficient water, while fish contributed to the process, reducing the remains to bones that dissolved within approximately five years.

On the seabed lies a vast expanse of leather shoes, preserved by tannic acid treatment, as silent witnesses to the tragedy. Surrounding the wreck are thousands of objects: bags, jewelry, pocket watches, plates, glasses, cutlery, tons of coal, and parts of the ship itself.

Investigations revealed that there was no 295-foot-long gash, as previously believed, but rather small breaches caused by the failure of rivets. The wreck, located 13,6 miles from the reported sinking point, confirms the survivors' accounts that the ship broke in two before descending to its watery grave.

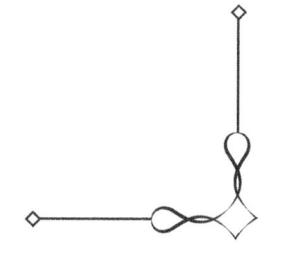

Titanic: The Silent Wreck's Voice Awakened

Ballard always regarded the Titanic as a cemetery, refusing to recover any objects. He left two commemorative plaques at the site: one in memory of the victims and the other asking future explorers to respect the wreck. However, his plea went unheeded.

Between 1987 and 1994, multiple expeditions retrieved hundreds of artifacts: plates, bottles, chandeliers, luggage, the cherub statue from the grand staircase, and the crow's nest bell. Many items, such as whistles, were restored; one was even connected to compressed air and blown in 1999 before a crowd of thousands.

A safe was also recovered in 1987, but it was found empty when opened. Today, these artifacts are displayed in various museums, while the Titanic still rests silently on the ocean floor, its secrets only partially revealed.

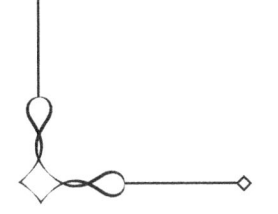

Sunken Memories: The Message of Oskar Holverson

One extraordinary item recovered from the Titanic wreck is a letter written on the ship's official stationery. This letter, penned by Oskar Holverson, a first-class passenger, was addressed to his mother on April 12, 1912, the day before the tragedy. Folded inside his notebook, the letter expressed affection and shared details about his onboard experience. Astonishingly, it withstood the extreme conditions of the ocean for over seventy years.

This precious document became the only letter written on Titanic stationery to survive the sinking. In 2017, it was auctioned for $166,000, a powerful testament to the personal stories intertwined with this maritime disaster. The letter offers a poignant glimpse into life aboard the ship before the tragedy unfolded.

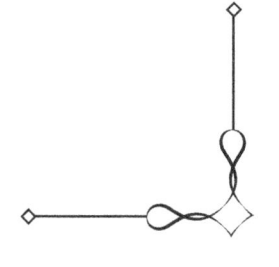

Legacy 1912: A Fragrance That Tells Stories of the Sea

From the depths of the ocean, the Titanic's wreckage unveiled an extraordinary find: a small leather bag containing 62 vials of perfume belonging to Adolphe Saalfeld, a first-class passenger. These oils, featuring rose, lavender, and bergamot notes, were intended for sale at a new perfume shop in the United States. Despite spending decades underwater, the vials remarkably preserved their original scents.

This discovery inspired the creation of the "Legacy 1912 Titanic Fragrance," which celebrates the elegance of a bygone era with its floral notes of lily of the valley and red thyme. This perfume is not merely a tribute to historical beauty but a way to relive the stories of those who traveled aboard the legendary ocean liner.

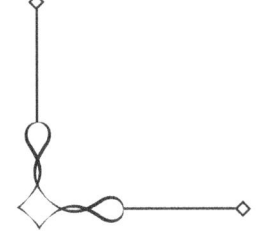

Love Carved on a Violin: The Story of Wallace

In April 1912, Wallace Hartley's violin played until the Titanic's final moments, delivering the melody of "Nearer My God to Thee." This treasured instrument, a gift from his fiancée Maria Robinson, was found strapped to Wallace's body, from which he never parted. An engraved silver plate on the violin's neck bore a heartfelt dedication from Maria, a poignant testament to their love.

After the tragedy, the violin was returned to Maria. Over time, it passed through various hands before being rediscovered in an attic in Lancashire. Following seven years of meticulous verification, it was authenticated in 2013 as "the Titanic violin." Displayed at the Belfast Museum, it was later auctioned for £900,000.

Crafted in Germany in 1880, this extraordinary relic remains steeped in history, carrying an unparalleled allure though forever silent.

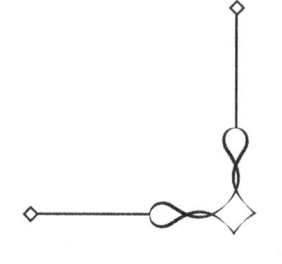

Memories of the Titanic: From the Grand Staircase to Virtual Reality

In 1995, James Cameron conducted multiple dives into the Titanic wreck to prepare for filming his iconic movie. In 1996, RMS Titanic, Inc. organized an expedition to recover a section of the ship's hull, later known as "The Big Piece."

This massive fragment, measuring 24 feet in length and 15 feet in height, was brought to the surface in 1998 and is now displayed at the Titanic Museum within the Luxor Hotel in Las Vegas. Visitors can also marvel at a life-sized replica of the first-class Grand Staircase, alongside numerous other original artifacts retrieved from the wreck.

In 2023, the latest expedition, led by Magellan, produced a high-definition 3D scan of the Titanic. Composed of over 700,000 assembled photographs, the result is a breathtakingly detailed three-dimensional model of the legendary ship.

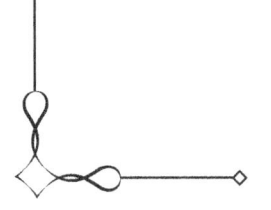

Corrosion and Silt: The Fate of a Legendary Ship

Sadly, the Titanic wreck can never be recovered. The bow plunged 59 feet into the silt upon impact, while the stern is almost completely destroyed. "Rusticles" are corroding the internal structure, causing the upper decks to progressively collapse as they slowly disintegrate.

The ship is now so fragile that any recovery attempt would destroy it entirely. The portion of the hull buried in the silt remains in unknown condition, but sonar images suggest that the bow is severely damaged and crumpled.

During the filming of *Ghosts of the Abyss*, James Cameron explored the cargo hold using remotely operated vehicles. However, only a few areas were accessible, confirming that the bow was filled with silt and likely deformed by the impact.

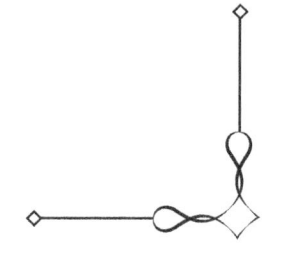

WHAT THEY DIDN'T TELL YOU

The Monumental Construction of the Titanic Set

For the filming of *Titanic*, 20th Century Fox built a colossal 16-hectare studio in Rosarito, Mexico, located directly by the sea. Filming began on September 18, 1996, and concluded on March 1, 1997, but the post-production process was lengthy and complex. The film's budget reached $200 million, surpassing even the cost of the original Titanic, which amounted to $7.5 million at the time (equivalent to approximately $180 million today).

The replica of the ship, constructed in just six months, was built to match the original dimensions, although some sections of the hull were scaled down to fit within a pool containing 64 million liters of water. Only the starboard side of the ship was built to protect the set from strong winds, and images of the port side were mirrored during editing.

Upon its initial release, the film grossed $1.8 billion, eventually reaching $2.2 billion with subsequent re-releases, making it the second highest-grossing movie in history, surpassed only by *Avatar*.

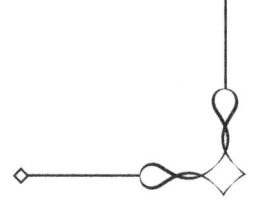

Technology and Historical Accuracy in the Production

The underwater scenes in *Titanic* combined real footage of the wreck with shots of a 1:20 scale model. These underwater sequences were filmed in a massive tank, where the ship's interiors were meticulously recreated using the original Titanic blueprints.

Furniture was treated with burning and sandblasting techniques to simulate 80 years of underwater wear. Some of the upholstery was even crafted by the same companies that had worked on the original Titanic in 1912. For scenes of the ship in motion, a 36-foot model was used, with special effects that included the sea, waves, and smoke.

Only two Titanic survivors watched the film: Eleanor Shuman, who attended the premiere and met James Cameron, and Michael Navratil, who saw it privately and wept throughout the screening.

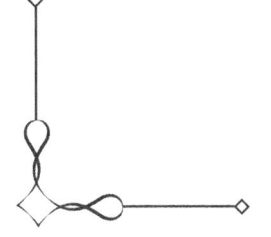

Between History and Fiction: The Secrets of Titanic in Cameron's Film

The characters of *Titanic*, Jack and Rose, are products of James Cameron's imagination, yet they incorporate references to historical and symbolic elements. Elderly Rose, portrayed by Gloria Stuart, is inspired by the life of Beatrice Wood, an American actress and sculptor who was not among the Titanic's passengers. However, there is a connection to reality in Joseph Dawson, a 23-year-old fireman buried in Halifax Cemetery, whose name appears on a gravestone following the disaster.

These historical and fictional details are also intertwined with the "Heart of the Ocean," a blue diamond created specifically for the film. Although it did not exist in reality, the jewel symbolizes the wealth aboard the ship, as exemplified by Lady Duff Gordon's pearl necklace, valued at $50,000, which was lost with the Titanic.

Through this blend of fiction and history, Cameron skillfully creates powerful and evocative symbolism, amplifying the emotional impact of the film.

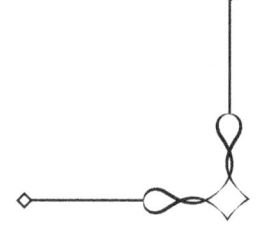

Poisoned Soup on Set: The Mystery That Shocked the Production

During the filming of *Titanic* in 1996 in Nova Scotia, the cast and crew experienced a surreal and dangerous event: they were poisoned with a powerful hallucinogen. The incident occurred when a group of criminals infiltrated the set and contaminated the clam chowder served to the crew with PCP, a dissociative hallucinogen also known as "angel dust."

More than 80 people, including cast and production members, began exhibiting severe confusion and bizarre behavior. Some requested a priest, others danced erratically, spoke to imaginary objects, or tried to harm themselves with pens.

James Cameron, realizing the gravity of the situation, induced vomiting in an attempt to rid himself of the drug's effects. While he managed to reduce the symptoms, his eyes remained bloodshot, a visible sign of the ordeal. Several people were hospitalized, but the perpetrators were never identified, leaving a shroud of mystery over who might have orchestrated the poisoning.

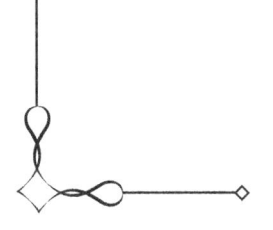

The Iconic Drawing Scene: DiCaprio, Cameron, and a Left-Handed Touch

Leonardo DiCaprio almost turned down the role of Jack Dawson in *Titanic*, initially hesitant to play the lead in a love story. It was James Cameron who convinced him, recognizing DiCaprio as the perfect face for a character destined to become iconic.

A fascinating detail about the scene where Jack draws Rose is that the hands we see on screen are not DiCaprio's but Cameron's. The director himself drew all the sketches in the film. Since Cameron is left-handed and DiCaprio is not, the scene was digitally flipped to appear authentic.

Although DiCaprio didn't create the drawings, he brought to life one of the most romantic and unforgettable moments in cinematic history. His performance made Jack Dawson a symbol of timeless romance, marking the beginning of DiCaprio's extraordinary international career.

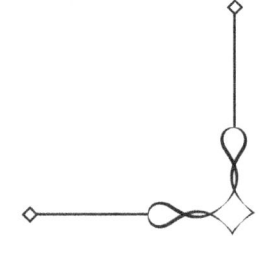

Cameron Responds: Why Jack Had to Die on the Titanic

James Cameron's *Titanic* not only told a heart-wrenching love story between Jack and Rose but also sparked years of debate over one technical detail: could both of them have survived on that infamous door?

Many believe Jack could have avoided freezing to death if only Rose had shared the makeshift raft. Photos and memes circulating online depict two people lying on the door.

James Cameron addressed these criticisms, explaining that the issue wasn't the space but the buoyancy. Even physics studies have explored the matter, calculating that the type of wood used would have influenced the outcome. In Mythbusters, the scene is recreated in water, showing that the door could have supported both. However, Cameron clarified that Jack had to die because it was written in the script.

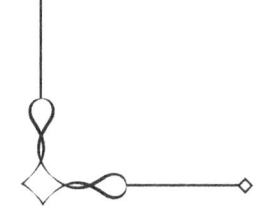

82

Titanic: The Myth of Unsinkability and the Hidden Truth

Now that we've explored some trivia about the film *Titanic* let's return to the real story of the ship. Contrary to popular belief, the Titanic was never officially declared "unsinkable" by the White Star Line, the company that built it. The myth of unsinkability actually originated from the media and technical articles of the time.

In 1911, *The Shipbuilder* magazine published an article highlighting the Titanic's technological innovations, such as its 16 watertight compartments and automatic closing doors, designed to seal in case of an emergency. The article described the ship as "practically unsinkable" due to these features.

From then on, journalists and the public began to label the Titanic as an "unsinkable" ship. This myth became tragically symbolic after the 1912 disaster when the ship struck an iceberg and sank, shattering this widely held perception.

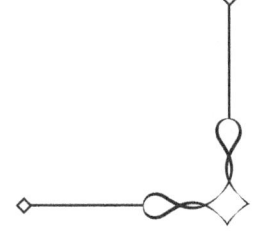

The Deception of Giants: The Insurance Scam Theory

Many conspiracy theories claim the White Star Line intended to swap the Titanic with the Olympic to commit insurance fraud. According to this theory, after an accident that damaged the Olympic in 1911, the company devised an audacious plan to sink the Titanic and collect the insurance money. The theorists suggest that by disguising the Olympic as the Titanic, they could sink an already compromised ship and secure a significant payout.

However, the ships exhibit substantial differences. For instance, the Titanic's A-deck promenade was enclosed to shield passengers from the elements, a feature absent in the Olympic. The Titanic's B-deck was extended to create luxury cabins and additional spaces, such as the Café Parisien, designed by Thomas Andrews and installed on the Olympic only in 1913. Lastly, both ships were insured for $5 million, but the construction costs exceeded $7.5 million, making the ship swap theory highly implausible.

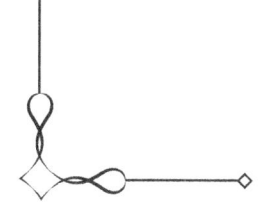

Masks at Sea: The Legend of Men in Disguise

During the Titanic disaster, a belief spread that many men dressed as women to secure spots on the lifeboats. This notion, fueled by contemporary newspapers, created an atmosphere of suspicion and discredit toward the few who desperately sought to survive. These baseless accusations led to ridicule for many, branding their acts of fear as a lifelong mark of disgrace.

However, only one third-class passenger, Daniel Buckley, admitted to donning a woman's shawl. He leaped aboard lifeboat No. 4, where, overwhelmed by anxiety, he broke into tears. Buckley claimed it was Madeline Astor, the wife of wealthy John Jacob Astor, who placed the shawl over his head.

His story, often overlooked, sheds light on the true human tragedy behind the sinking and the injustices perpetuated by the media.

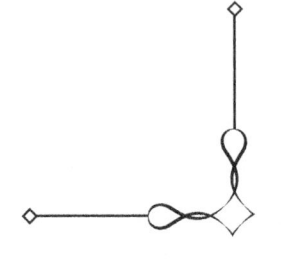

The Curse of the Mummy and the Titanic: Truth or Legend?

For many years, a belief persisted that the Titanic sank due to the "curse of an Egyptian mummy" hidden in the cargo hold. However, historical evidence entirely debunks this theory. The legend originated from an event aboard the ship itself. During a dinner, the renowned journalist W.T. Stead recounted the tale of an Egyptian mummy he had seen at the British Museum.

According to the story, anyone in possession of the mummy's sarcophagus would be plagued by misfortunes, accidents, and even death. When Stead tragically lost his life on the night of the sinking, the tale was sensationalized, fueling the belief that the mummy had been aboard the Titanic.

In reality, the sarcophagus never left the British Museum, where it remains on display today. The story was nothing more than one of the many myths born from the tragedy.

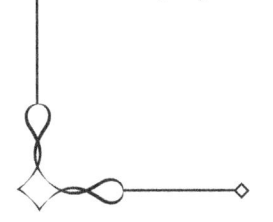

The Dual Mystery of the Titanic's Holes: Investigations on the Seafloor

In 1987, researchers observed two massive holes on both sides of the ship during an expedition to the Titanic wreck, sparking an intriguing theory. It was hypothesized that the sinking might have been caused by an internal explosion due to a fire in one of the coal bunkers.

This theory suggested that the fire had weakened the structure, leading to the ship's eventual breakage. However, further investigations disproved this hypothesis: the damages observed were above the waterline and did not match the patterns consistent with an explosion.

Instead, it was discovered that the holes resulted from the violent impact of the bow on the ocean floor. The immense pressure exerted during the ship's descent and the collision had bent the ship's structure, causing the observed damage.

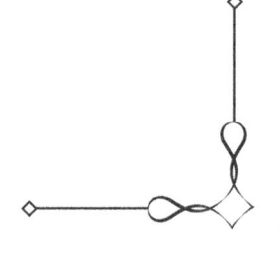

The Truth About the Titanic's Hull: The Metal Was Not Defective

In 1990, a portion of the Titanic's hull was recovered for analysis. Many had speculated that the metal used in the liner construction was of low quality, high in manganese sulfide, and therefore brittle.

However, tests conducted by engineer Tim Foecke of the National Institute of Standards and Technology revealed that the metal was nearly as strong as the material used in modern shipbuilding today. The Titanic's sinking, therefore, was not caused by the quality of the material. The true culprits were the ship's high speed, the collision with a 661.000 pounds iceberg, and the failure of the rivets.

Additionally, the Olympic, the Titanic's sister ship, was built with the same steel and operated for 25 years without significant structural issues, proving that the material was not defective. The damage to the Titanic was linked to its rivets, not the hull.

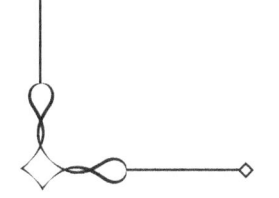

Fire or Iceberg? The Settled Controversy Over the Fate of the Great Ship

In 2017, a documentary based on the book Titanic Unseen reignited the theory that the Titanic's sinking was partially caused by a coal bunker fire. Some photographs of the ship departing from Belfast appeared to show a dark shadow near the point of impact with the iceberg, suggesting a more severe fire than initially thought, with temperatures reaching up to 1832°F.

However, subsequent analyses debunked this hypothesis: the shadow was merely a reflection from the dock, and tests on the rivets showed no significant weakening due to heat. Additionally, the fire was located in the sixth compartment, whereas the iceberg damaged the first five compartments.

The flooding alone would have compromised its buoyancy even if the fire had weakened the ship. Witnesses like Archibald Gracie, who used the first-class swimming pool, confirmed that the area showed no signs of damage or elevated temperatures.

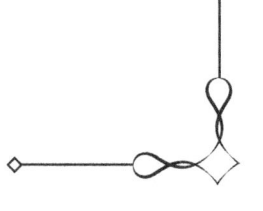

Endless Love: Elizabeth Isham's Heartbreaking Choice and Her Dog

The story of Elizabeth Isham is one of the most poignant connected to the sinking of the Titanic. She was traveling with her loyal Great Dane, and when offered a place on a lifeboat, she faced an agonizing decision. She was told her dog could not board the lifeboat, but Elizabeth, unable to part with her beloved companion, refused to leave him behind.

She chose to stay aboard the Titanic, perishing alongside him. Her body was later found in the icy waters of the Atlantic, embracing her dog. This tragic scene highlights the profound and unconditional bond between a human and their animal companion.

Elizabeth's choice represents an act of love and loyalty amid one of the greatest tragedies of the 20th century, making her story unforgettable.

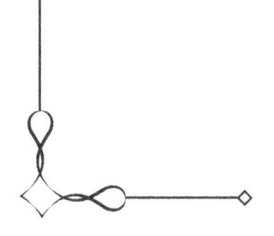

The Prophetic Wreck of the Titan: A Foreshadowing of the Titanic

In 1898, Morgan Robertson published *The Wreck of the Titan*, a story that seemed to eerily predict the Titanic disaster in 1912. The novella recounts the misfortunes of a sailor aboard the Titan, a massive ocean liner that, like its real-life successor, strikes an iceberg and sinks in the Atlantic Ocean.

Astonishingly, the details between the two ships are remarkably similar: both had three propellers and two masts, were deemed "unsinkable," and featured comparable dimensions (Titan: 800 feet, Titanic: 882 feet). Both departed in April, sank roughly 434 miles off Newfoundland, and had insufficient lifeboats.

Although the Titan was powered by steam and sail, the parallels between the two disasters are chilling. Following the Titanic's sinking, Robertson revisited his work, making the similarities even more striking.

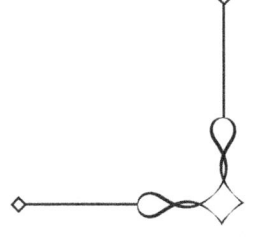

How an Unexpected Counterweight Saved Hundreds of Lives

While the stokers worked to extinguish the fire in the Titanic's coal bunker, they shoveled the burning coal directly into the boilers and moved the intact coal to an adjacent compartment. This massive material transfer created a list of approximately 2.5 degrees to port, as confirmed by passenger Lawrence Beesley.

Naval engineer Parks Stephenson, known for his collaboration on James Cameron's film, conducted studies and simulations suggesting that this accidental list actually helped stabilize the ship. Acting as a counterweight to the water flooding in on the starboard side, the slight tilt prevented the Titanic from capsizing quickly, allowing it to sink more slowly and upright.

According to his research, without this "stroke of luck," the ship would have capsized within an hour, rendering the lifeboats on the port side unusable and leading to an even greater catastrophe. For this reason, the list has been nicknamed "the guardian angel."

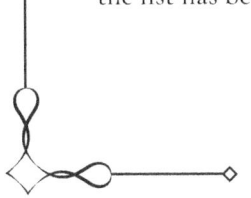

Beyond the Titanic: Forgotten Shipwrecks That Shook the World

Throughout history, the Titanic has been regarded as the greatest maritime disaster, but other shipwrecks have been equally devastating. On May 29, 1914, the Empress of Ireland sank in the St. Lawrence River after a collision, claiming the lives of 1,012 people. Although the death toll was lower than that of the Titanic, the impact was still immense.

Even more tragic was the fate of the Wilhelm Gustloff on January 30, 1945. This ship, carrying German refugees, was torpedoed by a Russian submarine, resulting in 7,000 deaths.

Finally, on December 21, 1987, the Philippine ferry Dona Paz collided with an oil tanker, catching fire and sinking rapidly. Although it was designed to carry 1,500 passengers, there were approximately 4,000 people on board that day. The fire and swift sinking left no survivors, making this disaster one of the deadliest ever recorded.

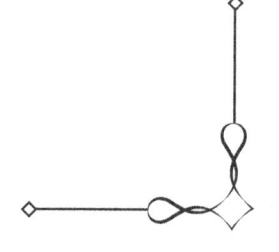

Lost Photographs and Documents: The Mystery of the Titanic's Propeller

One of the enduring mysteries surrounding the Titanic involves the configuration of its central propeller, as the wreck provides no conclusive evidence due to the mud covering it. Furthermore, no authentic photos of the Titanic's propeller exist; the known images are of its sister ship, the Olympic, which features a four-blade propeller.

However, a recent discovery at the Harland & Wolff shipyards has reshaped the narrative. A technical notebook indicates that while the Olympic initially had four blades, the Titanic was fitted with only three. After the Titanic's sinking, the Olympic was also temporarily equipped with a three-blade central propeller to test its efficiency before reverting to its original configuration.

Further evidence has emerged from a rare photo in Belfast during the Titanic's fitting-out phase, which clearly shows a three-blade central propeller on the dock. This confirms that this was the configuration used during its maiden voyage.

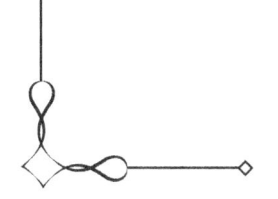

The Submerged Ear: The Device That Might Have Prevented the Tragedy

A lesser-known aspect of the Titanic involves a device called the "submerged ear," or the Fessenden Fathometer. This instrument was designed to detect underwater sounds and identify obstacles, particularly in conditions of low visibility, such as fog.

Invented by Reginald Fessenden, the Fathometer could identify other ships and potential hazards at sea. Some theories suggest that it may have been aboard the Titanic, but there is no definitive evidence to support this. Even if it had been installed, it is doubtful that it could have prevented the collision with the iceberg.

At the time, it was already known that the device was unsuitable for detecting icebergs, as it worked more effectively with metallic objects. The question of whether this instrument could have altered the Titanic's fate remains one of the many mysteries tied to the tragedy of that fateful night.

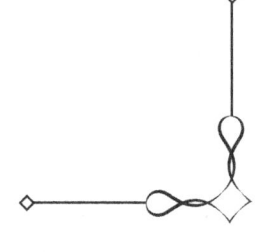

The Titan Submersible and the Deadly Allure of the Titanic

In June 2023, the Titan submersible tragically imploded while attempting to explore the wreckage of the Titanic, which sank in 1912, over 12,500 feet below the ocean's surface. Constructed from carbon fiber and titanium, the Titan was pushing the boundaries of modern deep-sea technology.

Six adventurers, including a billionaire, had each paid $250,000 for this once-in-a-lifetime experience aimed at reliving the history of the infamous shipwreck. However, the carbon fiber, which had not been fully tested for extreme depths, developed microscopic cracks.

These fissures ultimately led to the vessel's catastrophic implosion, destroying the submersible and claiming the lives of its occupants in mere milliseconds. This tragedy underscores the dangers of ocean exploration and the enduring fascination with the Titanic, a symbol of an era defined by daring adventures and unprecedented technological challenges.

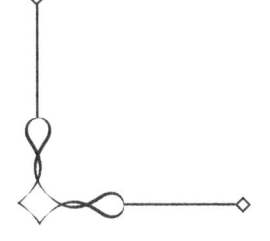

Queen Mary 2: The Ocean Giant Bridging Tradition and Modernity

The RMS Queen Mary 2, operated by Cunard, is the only modern ocean liner in regular service between Southampton and New York. Measuring 1132 feet in length, 134 feet in width, and 236 feet in height, it was the largest ship in the world from 2003 to 2006 until the arrival of Freedom of the Seas.

Its elegant silhouette, specifically designed to withstand the harshest conditions of the Atlantic, sets it apart from traditional cruise ships. Launched on September 25, 2003, the Queen Mary 2 made its maiden voyage on January 12, 2004, sailing from Southampton to Fort Lauderdale with 2,620 passengers on board.

In 2007, it embarked on its first circumnavigation of the globe, completing the journey in 81 days. With 15 restaurants and 5 swimming pools, the QM2 provides a refined travel experience, paying homage to Cunard's rich and historic tradition.

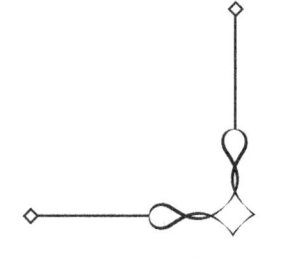

The Hidden Room on Deck D: The White Star Line's Secret Mystery

On Deck D, near the ship's hospital, lay a hidden room known only as "L" in the ship's blueprints. Kept secret by the White Star Line, it was a padded isolation cell meant for criminals or dangerous passengers on board. At the time, ships were the only means of intercontinental transport, and they had to be equipped to handle even the most critical situations.

If a passenger became problematic, they were first confined to a locked cabin. If this measure proved insufficient, they were taken to the ship's hospital for further isolation. As a last resort, the padded isolation cell was used in a small, 1.5 square meter room with canvas-lined walls designed to ensure maximum safety. This space was specifically created to maintain order on the open seas, far from the reach of any other authority.

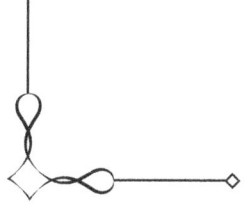

98

Jenny's Prophecy: The Cat Who Saved a Life on the Titanic

The story of Jenny, the Titanic's ship cat, blends reality and legend, captivating anyone who hears it. Jenny was brought aboard to hunt rodents but quickly bonded with fireman Jim Mulholland, who pampered her with the finest meals from the crew's kitchen. Pregnant at the time, Jenny gave birth on board, and only Jim was allowed near her kittens.

The day before the Titanic's departure, something extraordinary happened: under Jim's astonished gaze, Jenny carried her kittens one by one off the ship and left them on the dock. Superstitious by nature, Jim took the act as a bad omen. "Maybe she knows something we don't," he told his colleagues, deciding to leave the Titanic. On April 10, 1912, the ship sailed without him and never reached New York.

Thanks to his devotion to Jenny, Jim's life was spared, proving that love and affection can truly alter fate.

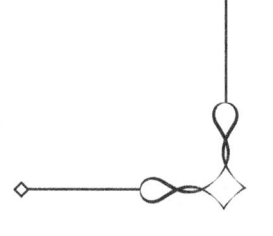

La Circassienne au Bain: The Story of the Titanic's Most Valuable Artifact

One of the most valuable objects lost in the sinking of the Titanic was the painting *La Circassienne au Bain* (1814) by Merry Joseph Blondel. This neoclassical masterpiece depicted a Circassian woman bathing and had been insured for $100,000 at the time, a sum equivalent to roughly $3 million today. Owned by Swedish magnate Mauritz Håkan Björnström Steffansson, who survived the disaster, the painting is considered the single most expensive item ever claimed in an insurance settlement related to the Titanic.

Although it was never recovered, the painting remains shrouded in mystery. Some say it was destined for a prestigious art gallery, but its fate was sealed in the depths of the Atlantic. This tragic loss has only amplified its legend, serving as a poignant symbol of the cultural treasures lost in the catastrophic sinking.

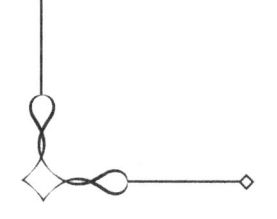

The End of an Era: The Rise and Fall of the White Star Line

The White Star Line's reputation took a severe blow after the Titanic disaster, requiring years to recover. To regain credibility, significant safety upgrades were made to the Olympic and Britannic. While the Olympic sailed for two decades, the Britannic sank during World War I, dealing another devastating setback to the company. Despite these losses, White Star continued operations, receiving two ships from the Germans renamed *Majestic* and *Homeric* as reparations for wartime sinkings. The *Majestic* became the new flagship, but financial mismanagement led to its decline.

In the 1920s, the company faced severe economic challenges and declared bankruptcy in 1932. The British government intervened, facilitating a merger with Cunard in 1933, forming the Cunard White Star Line. By 1947, Cunard fully absorbed the White Star Line, bringing an end to a historic era.

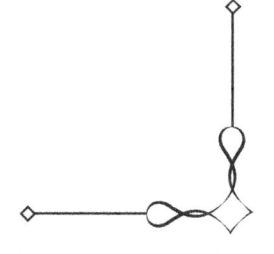

A Journey That Continues: Challenges and Discoveries

You have just completed a fascinating journey through 100 incredible and perhaps unexpected facts about the Titanic. But the voyage doesn't end here. Now it's time to dive even deeper into history, testing what you've learned and uncovering new details.

Get ready to challenge your memory, sharpen your observation skills, and discover even more curiosities.

In this special section, you'll find a series of challenges that will deepen your connection to the story of the Titanic.

Are you ready to put your knowledge to the test? Ready for an interactive journey that will take you once again through the corridors of that legendary ship? Then dive into the quizzes, hidden words, and an exclusive surprise we've prepared just for you.

Start your challenge by answering these questions. How much have you really learned about one of the most famous and tragic events in history? Test yourself and discover how much of a Titanic expert you are!

1. In what year did the Titanic sink?
   - A) 1905
   - B) 1910
   - C) 1912
   - D) 1920

2. How many smokestacks did the Titanic have?
   - A) 2
   - B) 3
   - C) 4
   - D) 5

3. Where was the Titanic when it struck the iceberg?
   - A) North Sea
   - B) Pacific Ocean
   - C) Baltic Sea
   - D) Atlantic Ocean

4. Who was the captain of the Titanic during its maiden voyage?
   - A) William Murdoch
   - B) Edward Smith
   - C) John Phillips
   - D) Thomas Andrews

5. What was the Titanic's final destination?
   - A) Boston
   - B) Halifax
   - C) New York
   - D) Washington

6. How many passenger classes were on the Titanic?
   - A) 2
   - B) 3
   - C) 4
   - D) 5

7. Where was the Titanic built?
   - A) London
   - B) Southampton
   - C) Belfast
   - D) Liverpool

8. When did the Titanic depart from Southampton?
   - A) April 10, 1912
   - B) April 12, 1912
   - C) April 14, 1912
   - D) April 15, 1912

9. What was the name of the Titanic's sister ship?
   - A) Carpathia
   - B) Olympic
   - C) Lusitania
   - D) Mauretania

10. What nickname was given to the Titanic before its maiden voyage?
    - A) "The Giant of the Sea"
    - B) "The Colossus of the Oceans"
    - C) "The Unsinkable"
    - D) "The Wonder of the Seas"

11. At what time of day did the Titanic hit the iceberg?
    - A) Early morning
    - B) Late afternoon
    - C) Midnight
    - D) Late night

12. How many hours after hitting the iceberg did the Titanic fully sink?
    - A) 1 hour
    - B) 2 hours
    - C) 2 hours and 40 minutes
    - D) 4 hours

13. Which ship first responded to the Titanic's SOS and rescued survivors?
    - A) Lusitania
    - B) Olympic
    - C) Britannic
    - D) Carpathia

14. How many of the Titanic's smokestacks were actually functional?
    - A) 2
    - B) 3
    - C) 1
    - D) 4

15. What was the estimated size of the iceberg that hit the Titanic?
    - A) 10 meters
    - B) 30 meters
    - C) 60 meters
    - D) 100 meters

16. Who was the Titanic's chief designer?
    - A) Bruce Ismay
    - B) John Jacob Astor
    - C) Thomas Andrews
    - D) William Pirrie

17. How many watertight compartments did the Titanic have?
    - A) 12
    - B) 14
    - C) 16
    - D) 18

18. Approximately how many passengers could the Titanic carry?
    - A) 1,500
    - B) 2,200
    - C) 2,500
    - D) 3,300

19. Approximately how many passengers survived the Titanic disaster?
    - A) 300
    - B) 705
    - C) 1,000
    - D) 1,500

20. Who was the president of the White Star Line during the Titanic's voyage?
    - A) J.P. Morgan
    - B) John Jacob Astor
    - C) Bruce Ismay
    - D) William Murdoch

21. Where was the Titanic's wreck discovered?
    - A) In the North Sea
    - B) Near Newfoundland
    - C) In the Azores
    - D) In the Bermuda Triangle

22. How many lifeboats were aboard the Titanic?
    - A) 12
    - B) 16
    - C) 20
    - D) 24

23. How many decks did the Titanic have?
    - A) 6
    - B) 7
    - C) 8
    - D) 9

24. In what year was the Titanic wreck discovered?
    - A) 1982
    - B) 1985
    - C) 1992
    - D) 2001

25. How long was the Titanic?
    - A) 259 meters
    - B) 269 meters
    - C) 279 meters
    - D) 289 meters

26. Which famous American millionaire died in the Titanic disaster?
    - A) John D. Rockefeller
    - B) Andrew Carnegie
    - C) John Jacob Astor
    - D) Cornelius Vanderbilt

27. Which band played as the Titanic sank?
    - A) The Bow Band
    - B) The Dining Orchestra
    - C) The Third-Class Band
    - D) The Captain's Orchestra

28. How many ships sent iceberg warnings to the Titanic that night?
    - A) 2
    - B) 4
    - C) 5
    - D) 6

29. Who built the Titanic?
    - A) Harland and Wolff
    - B) Lloyd's of London
    - C) White Star Line
    - D) Royal Dutch Shipbuilders

30. How many crew members were aboard the Titanic?
    - A) 500
    - B) 750
    - C) 900
    - D) 1,000

Now, to challenge your mind and observation skills in a different way, here's a test for your sharp eye and quick thinking. Hidden within the following grids are keywords related to the Titanic and its history. Find them all and complete the puzzle.

L.

B	D	I	L	U	H	P	P	N	Z	J	Q	P	G	Y	S	B	Z
S	K	Q	I	L	L	U	J	W	I	I	V	F	Q	E	K	W	Q
Z	S	W	R	G	M	S	T	A	D	B	E	F	I	L	X	A	G
Y	D	W	E	T	R	S	V	X	X	T	W	S	W	O	S	A	K
I	C	G	E	Y	W	E	P	I	G	R	B	Q	E	M	V	I	G
O	J	F	Y	R	W	T	B	I	P	N	W	Q	F	R	A	N	L
N	S	J	C	I	D	C	T	E	H	V	I	H	C	T	D	A	R
H	S	D	G	H	S	N	Y	C	C	S	A	K	L	T	M	T	M
C	A	F	R	P	F	R	A	H	C	I	R	A	N	I	F	I	V
O	L	U	R	A	Q	H	M	I	E	A	N	E	D	I	Y	S	L
D	C	D	V	R	W	P	E	R	V	T	R	S	T	E	S	U	E
R	I	O	X	G	I	D	I	L	I	Q	M	P	Q	S	D	L	V
U	S	T	H	E	W	X	E	C	U	I	I	D	A	Q	I	U	I
M	R	Z	O	L	X	W	W	F	T	C	K	M	X	T	B	S	Q
N	I	C	Y	E	P	N	L	H	S	O	S	W	I	B	H	P	L
D	F	F	Z	T	W	Z	M	Q	T	I	I	E	E	Z	X	I	B
U	C	I	N	A	T	I	T	A	A	T	X	V	R	V	Y	T	A
Q	C	A	R	L	L	U	D	F	D	J	H	A	G	T	M	E	T

ANDREWS ATLANTIC CARPATHIA
EDWARD FIRST CLASS ICEBERG
LIFEBOATS LUSITANIA MURDOCH
RESCUE SINKING SISTER SHIP
SMITH TELEGRAPH TITANIC

2.

L	B	M	A	D	G	S	O	U	L	V	C	P	M	S	S	K	I
M	V	U	X	E	I	C	O	M	P	A	R	T	M	E	N	T	S
V	P	A	S	S	E	N	G	E	R	S	K	E	D	W	D	L	E
R	F	Z	P	R	A	T	S	E	I	I	H	W	R	J	U	Z	G
D	M	F	Y	M	D	H	H	X	E	E	H	E	A	Q	P	H	A
I	C	H	I	M	N	F	Y	U	A	I	C	I	S	D	D	H	Y
Z	Y	P	U	T	U	I	C	Z	U	K	C	I	P	M	Y	L	O
S	F	X	S	C	V	S	U	C	T	D	B	B	O	B	A	X	V
B	R	P	U	R	F	N	L	N	O	B	Y	T	C	I	M	I	I
T	I	S	R	R	M	M	A	R	D	U	S	Z	Z	L	S	V	A
H	P	T	V	U	P	G	M	R	A	A	L	Q	O	M	Z	L	R
F	P	V	L	O	R	W	Z	N	I	W	Z	O	A	Y	S	M	U
Z	L	D	Y	O	M	R	V	L	I	T	V	Y	R	A	G	R	G
E	C	H	M	C	W	Z	E	X	B	A	H	N	N	I	M	R	U
P	W	M	E	O	D	B	P	I	K	I	T	D	G	I	W	T	A
Z	I	T	B	Z	Y	K	S	B	F	T	A	P	S	F	Z	R	N
G	F	Q	T	H	I	R	D	C	L	A	S	S	A	C	Y	N	I
U	R	F	R	Y	X	A	S	D	S	J	Q	M	V	C	Q	P	F

BELFAST
CHIMNEY
ISMAY
PASSENGERS
THIRD CLASS

BOW
COMPARTMENTS
MORGAN
RESCUE
WHITE STAR

CAPTAIN
INAUGURAL VOYAGE
OLYMPIC
SURVEY
WRECK

Answers to the Questions:

1. C) 1912
2. C) 4
3. D) Atlantic Ocean
4. B) Edward Smith
5. C) New York
6. B) 3
7. C) Belfast
8. A) April 10, 1912
9. B) Olympic
10. C) "The Unsinkable"
11. D) Late Night
12. C) 2 hours and 40 minutes
13. D) Carpathia
14. B) 3
15. B) 30 meters
16. C) Thomas Andrews
17. C) 16
18. B) 2,200
19. B) 705
20. C) Bruce Ismay
21. B) Near the coast of Newfoundland
22. C) 20
23. D) 9
24. B) 1985
25. B) 269 meters
26. C) John Jacob Astor
27. B) The onboard orchestra
28. D) 6
29. A) Harland and Wolff
30. D) 1,000

As a final gift for your journey through the history of the Titanic, we want to offer you something special. Scan the QR code below to download an exclusive digital book filled with authentic testimonies from survivors.

You'll be able to immerse yourself in their stories, relive those moments of terror, and hear the voices of those who survived that icy night.

This is our small token of appreciation for traveling with us through the facts and secrets of the Titanic.

As you close this book, perhaps you can still hear the distant echo of waves crashing against the Titanic's hull, this legendary ship that has never truly ceased sailing in our hearts and minds. Every story, every fact, every character you've encountered within these pages has helped weave the fabric of a myth that still endures today.

We've journeyed together through the birth of a giant, shared in its glory, and finally, mourned its fall. Yet, like the Titanic itself, the stories we tell never truly sink. They continue to live, floating within our collective memory, ready to be told again and again.

If this journey has touched your heart, if it has fascinated you, or if you've discovered something new that you didn't know before, we have a small favor to ask: leave your review on Amazon. Your words are not only a way to share what you've felt but also a means to help other readers embark on this extraordinary voyage.

And so, just as every passenger of the Titanic left their mark on history, you too can be part of this adventure with your review.

Thank you for sailing with us, and remember: the story of the Titanic is never just a tale of the past. It is a story that lives within each of us.

Printed in Dunstable, United Kingdom